The 1-Page Budgeting Plan

Become Debt Free, Accumulate Savings, Build Wealth Investing, and Live Life on Your Terms

By Zoe McKey

rendering medical, legal or other professional advice or services. If professional assistance is required, the services of a competent professional person should be sought. The author shall not be liable for damages arising herefrom. The fact that an individual, organization of website is referred to in this work as a citation and/or potential source of further information does not mean that the author endorses the information the individual, organization to website may provide or recommendations they/it may make. Further, readers should be aware that Internet websites listed in this work might have changed or disappeared between when this work was written and when it is read.

For general information on the products and services or to obtain technical support, please contact the author.

CREATED BY

ZOE MCKEY

SELF-DISCOVERY

~Starter Kit~

Thank you for choosing my book! I would like to show my appreciation for the trust you gave me by giving a **FREE GIFT** for you!

For more information visit www.zoemckey.com.

The kit shares *10 key practices to help you to:*

- *discover your true self,*

- *find your life areas that need improvement,*

- *find self-forgiveness,*

- *become better at socializing,*

- *lead a life of gratitude and purpose.*

The kit contains extra actionable worksheets with practice exercises for deeper learning.

Table of contents...

Introduction

Imagine having an awesome GPS. It finds you the best routes every time, calculates every aspect of your trip, and gives you astonishingly accurate data on your ETA, obstacles, checkpoints, police—everything. But you don't know the destination you want to go to. You can have the best GPS, but without a clear destination in mind, it is useless. On the other hand, you can have the most mind-blowing, beautiful destination in mind, but if you don't have the GPS—or heck, at least a plain paper map—you won't know how to get to the place of your dreams. A good GPS and a well-defined, intriguing destination are both needed to have the trip of your life. Similarly, you need a good budgeting method and clearly defined financial goals to reach financial freedom.

Do you have audacious plans in your mind? Wild dreams? Fifty countries to visit? Or maybe you dream of having a calm and cozy home where a lack of money is never a problem? I hear you. It's so heartwarming to daydream about palm trees, cozy mountain cottages, a full fridge… *I wonder when I will get there?* We ask this question and then return to the grind. Weeks are turning into months, months into years. We don't understand why our dreams are still unfulfilled. We work so hard! Life is unfair! Why?

Why? That's a great question to ask.

Why is it that we run low on cash each month? Why is it that, although we work 8-10 hours a day, we seem to be going nowhere? Why do we lack direction?

"If I asked you, 'Do you know what your financial goals are?' could you give me a quick, no-brainer answer? The majority of people can't. If I asked you, 'Do you know where your money goes each month?' could you tell me? Most people couldn't. Do you have some kind of system in which you manage and track your income and expenses? You guessed it right, most people don't know. Okay, so you don't have a destination and you don't have a GPS either, and you're surprised you're not going anywhere?" said my financial mentor, shaking his head in disapproval. That's when my financial journey started changing for good.

I was 25 and, I must say, extremely lucky to have been mocked about my financial illiteracy so early on. To be fair, I had a vague money-tracking system. I tracked all my expenses and income in a little pink book. I wasn't prioritizing or making smart decisions, rather just making sure to not run low on cash before the month ended. Whenever I saw that I was licking the bottom of my money tank, I pulled the hand brake and I lived on cheap salami and bread until the next month's wages came in. Sometimes this happened 10 days beforehand.

"Failing to plan is planning to fail."

My financial mentor, let's call him Midas, had a lot of knowledge about money. He could talk for hours about the importance of having clear financial goals; he had deep knowledge about where the money is coming from and where it goes, or as he put it, having a coordinated and comprehensive system for financial decision-making. To put it simply, look at where you are now, plan for where you want to be in the future, and considering these two data points, create a long-term financial plan for yourself. He told me about savings accounts, retirement funds, investment accounts, ETFs... *WTF?*

I had no clue. And I am not the only one. According to the National Association of Personal Financial Advisors, almost 60% of US adults don't have any financial plan. NAPFA also shows that 39% of US adults don't have any other type of savings than pensions. 50% of Americans with children don't have a will, and two out of five Americans would give Cs, Ds, or Fs to their level of financial awareness.[i] And ladies, I have some bad news for us. When it comes to financial savvy, we have some catching up to do. A recent survey by Country Financial found that 23.6% of women never ask for financial advice compared to just 15.2% of men. And when women do ask for advice, it is mostly for retirement planning. But still, only 37% of women asked about retirement savings compared to 45% of men.

It's no unknown fact that women live longer than men. In fact, we live on average five years longer than men! So shouldn't we be asking a little bit more about retirement financial planning since we'll be living longer? I think so! But still, women are afraid to ask.

These are scary numbers, especially because the United States is one of the world's most developed and educated countries. Imagine the percentages in countries where education is less accessible and where it's even harder to make ends meet.

Some people are repelled by learning about the "dirty money." To some, money is the direct derivation of evil. Money is neither good nor evil—in fact, money on some level is an illusion. It's a shape-shifter, either on paper or in a combination of zeros and ones in a computer system. That, and the emotions we attribute to it.

How would you feel if you could wake up each day knowing that you can satisfy not only your basic needs but you could have the freedom to travel, to fulfill your goals and dreams? If you could help those your love when they are in need? If you could feel safe, secure, free, and ultimately alive? Ultimately, it's not the money that we are after, but the feelings and emotions we can enjoy thanks to money.

I know it is not glamorous what I'm saying. I know it sounds better to say that money doesn't buy happiness. But it can buy time, freedom, peace of mind, experiences—which all lead to happiness. And at the end of the day, you either use money or it uses you. Don't let the shape-shifter win! Let's learn to domesticate it and put it to work for us!

What does it mean to have a financial plan?

First of all, a financial plan offers you transparency. Planning your life goals and desires financially will help you see the big picture of how and when you can achieve them. You'll also have clear knowledge about your daily, monthly, and yearly expenditures.

You'll be able to see how and where you can cut expenses to regroup your money for a better cause. By analyzing your spending habits, needs, and wishes, you can develop a realistic budget that you can stick to. You can cultivate trust and respect toward yourself when you see the first fruits of your financial discipline.

You can always turn to a professional financial planner to help you map out your finances. A professional will be able to determine your net worth, give you information about life-planning assumptions like inflation rates, rates of return, saving ratios, etc. If you're thinking about investing, a professional can help you find the opportunities that best fit your needs (low-risk, high-interest). Be cautious about who you choose to be your financial advisor, though. Make sure they provide fiduciary service. Don't buy into every "just now, just for you" deals. Having a financial advisor doesn't mean you can take your hands off your financial self-education. You should always be aware of what's happening with your money and understand the process you get yourself into.

I know, learning real-life finances by yourself is tough. You may wonder—just like I did—why didn't they teach me this in school? The question is legit. Our education failed in preparing us to handle our financial adulthood. According to Money Savvy Youth, only 59% of young adults pay their bills on time. 81% of college students underestimate the time they could pay off their student loans in.[ii] 76% of families live paycheck to paycheck, and 27% have zero savings.[iii] Our education system still doesn't care about improving these crazy statistics. It is not surprising that our financial awareness turned out to be as bad as our parents'—that's what we learned.

It is up to us now to improve the knowledge we lack. Schools supposedly teach us how to make good money, but they never teach how to manage it. If you want to be financially (care)free, you have to learn it for yourself. You don't need to become the weird finance geek who tosses papers and tax reports and tracks the stock market with bloodshot eyes all day. Life is too short for that. But the longer you wait to get a financial life, the harder it will be to fulfill your goals. You'll have less time. You might hope for a better economy, a larger paycheck, *and then* you will get your stuff together. Don't forget, as the number of your years increases and your paycheck, so will your expenses. Each day you delay to start devising and following a financial plan, the compound interest on your debts will grow bigger, the compound interest you could cash in on your savings and investments will bear fruits later, and you'll keep spinning in the rat race without a GPS or a destination for longer.

So get started today! This book will help you realize your wildest financial dreams.

Chapter 1: Find Out Where You Want to Go

What Are Your Financial Goals?

Financial goals can be anything from buying a new phone to paying off your college debt to achieving financial freedom. You may want to move into a bigger house or move out from your parents' house. Maybe you want to quit working for a year and have an epic, wild backpacking trip. Do you have a charitable heart? You can help more buying food for ten than preparing food for one. Do you love spending time with your family? Well, guess what buys you time?

Not everybody aims to be a millionaire. It is not easy to become one—definitely not as easy as some may present it. Some people value other stuff more than money. There's nothing wrong with that. But let's face it, regardless of where our values lie, we can explore them much better if we have money. Financial goals don't have to be strictly purchasable. Having time for a weekend at your seaside house with your family doesn't need hard cash per se, but hiring someone to do your work for a few days—or affording to take an unpaid vacation—is also an implicit cost.

The first step on this journey is to identify and jot down all your desires that are related to your finances. Then, step two is turning them into actual, achievable goals by attaching a dollar value next to them.

Let's see a few examples.

1. Pay off your credit card debt after college.

A college student graduates with at least $3000 in credit card debt—on average. If we assume they only make the minimum payment each month, it will take them about 20 years and more than $4000 *in interest only* to pay off the debt. And this is a best-case scenario—we assumed no additional debt is added. The lesson: Pay off your debts as quickly as possible to use your money to gain more rewarding prospects.

2. Buy a new home.

First-time home buyers paid a median price of $203,700 in 2019.[iv] To qualify for a loan for that home, they had to make a down payment of between 10-20% of the full price. They also had to pay 1-5% of the home's price as a closing cost to the bank. This means that this first-time home buyer had to have up to $41,540 saved up for the down payment and another $2,037-$10,185 for the closing cost. (These numbers can be higher or lower depending on the region, the deal, the condition of the house, etc.)

3. Build an emergency fund.

While this is not a sexy financial goal like saving for a new fast car, I really hope some of you have it on your bucket list. Experts suggest that a healthy emergency fund consists of at least three and up to six months' worth of living expenses. Having a safety cushion of this size will give you peace of mind when dealing with future unexpected events.

Before we start collecting your financial goals, let's consider a few cautionary aspects. I daydream of a lovely wooden-stone cottage in the middle of the wild woods of... wherever—Canada, say. I would like this cottage to be ultra-modern yet rustic, I'd like to have kittens, and I'd like a coffee corner. However, I must resign to the fact that I don't have the financial means for it –

for now. So, based on my prospects of today, it isn't realistic to budget for that, considering that I have so many other things to budget for.

Many people who try setting up a financial plan get off track by setting unrealistic goals. To be able to create realistic and achievable goals, you need to examine two things:

- Your income.
- Your expenses.

Income:

Income is your monthly salary, your passive income stream (royalties, interests, shares, dividends, etc.), bonuses, inheritance, or winnings. Everything that adds money to your tab (before taxes) is considered your income.

Expenses:

Everything that takes away from your tab is an expense. I distinguish three types of expenses.

- Essentials: food, housing-related costs, utility bills, debt payments, and transportation.

- Personal expenses: cable TV, coffee in a café, makeup, clothing, gym memberships, dining out, other memberships... In my assessment, extra luxury choices in your essential expenses are rather personal expenses. For example, renting an apartment in the city center to avoid commuting is not a luxury. If you rent the rooftop apartment for a better view with an extra 10% rental fee, that's a luxury.

- Savings. Having savings can grant you a feeling of safety. You can be sure that if a car hits you, if you fall ill, or if you just need to aid a friend last minute, money won't be a problem. The most common expenses in the "savings" category are: savings plans, emergency funds, and retirement savings.

Task 1:

Write a list of your income and expenses. This is a very important step, and the rest of this book will depend on how well you collected them.

Take two pieces of paper; one for your income, the other for your expenses. You can also do this digitally. Then use a different Google Sheet for each. Try to put the exact number of fixed expenses like subscription fees, membership fees, and utility bills. If you don't know the exact amount you spend on food, for example, just estimate a number. Don't try to separate the expenses into essentials, personal expenses, and savings yet. Just jot everything down that comes to mind.

Unfortunately, for most of us, collecting our income takes like five minutes at best. There are only a few—or just a single—income streams. The number of expenses on our list overpowers the number of income streams. But that's not an issue as long as the monetary value of our expenses doesn't surpass the monetary value of our income.

Add up your income streams and expenses and see which one is bigger. If the income, you're on board. If it's the expenses, that's a problem, especially if they don't include any savings. In this case, you have two simple options: you either need to increase your income (harder) or cut your expenses (simpler—not necessarily easier).

To help you, I created a quick list to collect your income and expenses. The items added to each might not reflect your specific situation, so feel free to adjust this list on your paper:

INCOME (what you cash in monthly)

-Salary + bonuses: _____

-Income from a second job: _____

-Interest on your savings: _____

-Royalties: _____

-Income from investments (cash you take out from your portfolio instead of reinvesting): _____

- Scholarship, government aid: _____

-Other: _____

TOTAL INCOME PER MONTH: _____ (before taxes)

EXPENSES (what you spend each month)

-Federal, state, local income tax: _____

-Tax on interest and investment income: _____

-Mortgage: _____

-Other type of debt payment (car loan, student loan, credit card debt): _____

-Rent and utilities: _____

-IRA and 401(k) contributions: _____

-Groceries: _____

-Subscriptions (gym, cell phone, TV, etc.): _____

-Social life expenses (night out, eating out, happy hours etc.):

-Clothing expenses: _____

-Personal hygiene: _____

-Commuting (gas, public transportation etc.): _____

-Insurance payment (health, homeowner, disability, car, life): _____

-Home maintenance: _____

-Child care: _____

-Hobbies: _____

-Vacation: _____

-Investment: _____

- Other: _____

TOTAL EXPENSES PER MONTH:

_____

Before we move on, let me ask you a few questions. Are you currently debt free? Do you have a five-figure or six-figure income? Do you invest with success? Do you save/ successfully invest 30-50% of your total income? If you answered yes to all these questions, this book is not for you. You, my friend, are exceptional at making and managing money. Please, *you* contact *me* to teach me your secrets. If, however, you answered no to any of the four questions above, keep reading. This book might help you.

Do you want to accumulate savings for your dreams, wishes, and future needs? If you answered yes to this question, you need a budget.

Budgeting, while it's quite simple, is not easy. It involves painful compromises, difficult choices, and many renunciations. However, as long as your financial goals are realistic, the effort will be worthwhile. When I say realistic, I mean realistic in the present. If you make $50,000 a year, trying to save up for a private jet is not the most realistic goal. If, however, for any reason your circumstances change in two years and you start making $500,000 a year, that jet might not be so far fetched. In this case, you need to reevaluate and adjust the budget you set up today and plan your finances accordingly. But start with what you have today and set realistic goals for real success. In a few pages you'll learn how.

If information was the only thing you needed to achieve everything you want financially, the world would be filled with private-jet–flying millionaires. Reading more about finances after a certain point won't make a change. Taking action will. This being said, basic but sturdy financial literacy is necessary to understand why, in fact, budgeting works, and what the financial accelerators and dead-end streets are.

Making more money won't necessarily make you *wealthier*. First, you need to learn to handle what you have now. More money won't help you be better with money.

This book isn't only about teaching you how to budget money. Rather, it's about how to get to where you truly want to be in life from where you are today. Whatever that means; achieving financial independence or securely storing cash in a savings account. You need to know what your goal is, clearly, because you need to take different routes to achieve these two outcomes. To simply accumulate cash for peace of mind, you need to save as much as possible on a month-to-month basis. The upside of this goal is that you have access to liquid cash anytime. The downside is that you lose approximately 3% of the buying power of that cash to inflation. If you want to achieve financial independence and accelerate your wealth building, you need to reinvest a portion of what you earn to multiply it. The upside of this route is the chance of getting out of the rat race. The downside, of course, is the volatility of the stock market and the increased risk of actually losing money. I will talk more in depth about investing later.

How would it feel like to have knowledge and experience about handling money well? If it wouldn't be a source of stress anymore, but rather one of excitement and hope? For that, we need to know what exactly you want to achieve financially in the next one, five, ten, and twenty years.

Without further ado, please use the template below to collect your financial goals.

My Financial Goals

This is what I want to achieve in 1 year:

-

-

-

This is what I want to achieve in 5 years:

-

-

-

This is what I want to achieve in 10 years:

-

-

-

This is what I want to achieve in 20 years:

-

-

-

Take some time to fill the chart above. Think well and think carefully. This step is very important for setting your budget up with the correct amounts you need to save. Anything from buying a new car in three years to having a safety cushion of $50,000 in five years can be a legitimate goal. You know your income. You don't need to have three goals for each section. If you have only one goal, it's cool. Having four to five goals is also cool, as long as they are realistic.

Done? Okay. Let's go to step two of goal setting.

Task 2:

Make your goals SMART.

SMART is an abbreviation for Specific, Measurable, Achievable, Relevant, and Time-framed. Your financial goals should be inserted in the SMART framework. Make sure your financial goals have a specific dollar amount and a deadline assigned to them. I will provide you with an example of a goal and lead it through these five aspects.

Let's say one of your one-year goals is to take a two-week trip to Europe to celebrate your ten-year marriage anniversary. How could this trip be achieved?

Let's say you've looked into dates, flights, and accommodations, and it would cost $3000. You want to go next year—in twelve months. Ergo, you have twelve months to save $3000. This means you have to save $250/month. (For simplicity, I don't count in inflation, currency exchange, and other factors.) Do you find saving this amount realistic? Can you spare this money?

If not, you have to reevaluate the goal, the deadline, or the budget. Whether you start to save earlier, whether you change the destination, it's up to you. If you do find saving that amount to be realistic for you, congratulations! You just set a SMART goal.

The goal is specific: a two-week trip to Europe.

It is measurable: $3000.

If you can save $250 a month, it means the goal is achievable.

It is also relevant. You don't have a ten-year marriage anniversary every day, after all. Finally, the goal is time-framed: in twelve months.

Your turn. Let's plan for your goals. I created worksheets for short-term goals and long-term goals. You can fill up as many as you wish, but remember, stay realistic with your plans.

SMART for goals with a one-year deadline:

Goal 1: _____

    Specific: _____

    Measurable: _____

    Achievable: _____

    Relevant: _____

    Time-framed: _____

Goal 2: _____

      Specific: _____

      Measurable: _____

      Achievable: _____

      Relevant: _____

      Time-framed: _____

Goal 3: _____

      Specific: _____

      Measurable: _____

      Achievable: _____

      Relevant: _____

      Time-framed: _____

SMART for goals with a five-year deadline:

Goal 1: _____

      Specific: _____

      Measurable: _____

Achievable: _____

Relevant: _____

Time-framed: _____

Goal 2: _____

    Specific: _____

    Measurable: _____

    Achievable: _____

    Relevant: _____

    Time-framed: _____

Goal 3: _____

    Specific: _____

    Measurable: _____

    Achievable: _____

    Relevant: _____

    Time-framed: _____

SMART for goals with a ten-year deadline:

Goal 1: _____

       Specific: _____

       Measurable: _____

       Achievable: _____

       Relevant: _____

       Time-framed: _____

Goal 2: _____

       Specific: _____

       Measurable: _____

       Achievable: _____

       Relevant: _____

       Time-framed: _____

Goal 3: _____

       Specific: _____

       Measurable: _____

       Achievable: _____

       Relevant: _____

       Time-framed: _____

SMART for goals with a twenty-year deadline:

Goal 1: _____

      Specific: _____

      Measurable: _____

      Achievable: _____

      Relevant: _____

      Time-framed: _____

Goal 2: _____

      Specific: _____

      Measurable: _____

      Achievable: _____

      Relevant: _____

      Time-framed: _____

Goal 3: _____

Specific: _____

Measurable: _____

Achievable: _____

Relevant: _____

Time-framed: _____

Make sure everything is filled out and that everything is achievable within today's measures. If you're planning on starting to invest, you may reevaluate these goals later. Good investments can accelerate our goals or make it possible to add new goals.

To help you with transparency, I added a chart below from the book *Get a Financial Life* by Beth Kobliner. (You must forgive me, I bought the book used—which is a good way to save money, by the way—so the chart has some notes. Focus on the message.)

Figure 2-1

HOW MUCH DO YOU NEED TO SAVE EACH MONTH TO MEET YOUR GOALS?

Look across the top row and find the dollar amount that corresponds to your goal. Now look down the far-left column and locate the number of years in which you hope to achieve your goal. The point at which your goal and the number of years intersect is the amount you need to save each month.*

Years to Reach Your Goal	YOUR SAVINGS GOAL										
	$1,000	$2,000	$3,000	$5,000	$7,000	$10,000	$20,000	$30,000	$50,000	$70,000	$100,000
1	$85	$169	$254	$423	$607	$845	$1,691	$2,536	$4,227	$6,067	$8,454
2	43	86	129	215	301	429	859	1,288	2,146	3,005	4,293
3	29	58	87	145	203	291	581	872	1,453	2,035	2,906
4	22	44	66	111	155	221	443	664	1,107	1,549	2,214
5	18	36	54	90	126	180	360	539	899	1,259	1,798
6	15	30	46	76	106	152	304	456	761	1,065	1,521
7	13	26	40	66	93	132	265	397	662	927	1,324
8	12	24	35	59	82	118	235	353	588	823	1,176
9	11	21	32	53	74	106	212	318	531	743	1,061
10	10	19	29	48	68	97	194	291	485	679	969

*The goals listed across the top row of the table are in constant dollars. This means that if your goal is to buy a car in five years that's equivalent to a $20,000 car today, you need to set aside $360 every month to end up with a sum that has the right purchasing power ($20,000 today is equal to roughly $17,000 five years from now). In other words, you don't have to worry about inflation eroding the value of the $20,000; the table factors it in for you.

Picture 1: How much to save each month to achieve your goals.

What can we see on this chart? The horizontal row shows different amounts of savings goals. The vertical row shows the number of years we plan to get there. For example, if we want to save $50,000 in five years we need to save $899 a month. If you make the calculation 899x12 (the number of months a year) x5 (the number of years we want to accumulate the savings), it equals $53,940. How come?

The author explains that the top row's dollars are constant. You don't need to worry about inflation eroding the value of your savings as the suggested amount of savings already took that into account. We want to focus to have the buying power of $50,000 in five years. The table was calculated with a 3% inflation rate and a 4% interest rate earned before taxes.

Use this chart to put a price tag and a monthly savings tag on your goals. Let's look at a practical example. If your one-year goals require you to save up $3,000, your five-year goals $50,000, your ten-year goals an additional $20,000, you'll need to save $254 per month for the first, $899 for the second, and $194 for the third. This would mean $1347 in savings per month to be sure that, if nothing changes (which, of course, is impossible), you'll have $3,000 to spend in one year, $50,000 to spend for your five-year goals, and $20,000 for your ten-year goals.

This is very literal and simplistic thinking, not considering any market variables, but it can give you an idea of how much money you need right now to consider your goals realistic.

Please make sure you complete each exercise before you move on with the reading. In the next few chapters we'll dig deeper into each financial variable you need to know more about to make informed financial decisions for your future.

Chapter 2: Financial Myths and Traps

Let's take a moment to talk about what money myths are. As you grow up, you are constantly fed different ideas about money and finances. Since finances aren't often taught in school, you are left mirroring what your family has told you. And unfortunately, our families often aren't the best examples of how we should build wealth. Unless you grew up in a household which made great financial choices, mirroring your family's financial path can lead to you having a negative view of how money works.

The secret to making your wealth is not the amount of money you have, but the mindset toward it. Let's put this into perspective ...

If you were a billionaire who'd lost almost all of their money, but was left with two million dollars, what would you think? You would think you were poor! Two million seems like a huge amount of money, but compared to billions, it is nothing. If an actual billionaire lost all their money, they wouldn't think they were poor. They would think of strategies to recreate their wealth. This is what we call a millionaire mindset. Money is just a tool; the real power resides in the knowledge of how to create money.

Most people believe having a few thousand dollars is successful. If you want to be wealthy, you need to change your mindset about money.

Let's see how money myths can hurt our wealth and lead us (further) into debt. Day in and day out, we tell ourselves lies to justify our bad financial decisions. Below, I will highlight some of the most common money myths we all find ourselves using.

"It was on sale. I saved money."

One day, I went out shopping with my friends at the nearest mall. We were walking through the mall when my friends started getting really excited. I looked in the direction they were staring and found the sign: "Big Sale, Up to 75% Off!" I immediately went to the store with them and started looking through the racks. When I found a dress I had been eyeing in the window, I looked at the price tag.

It was originally $200, but was now on sale for $50! I could not pass up the deal and quickly purchased the dress.

Looking back on that incident, I realize how silly it is that we all purchase so much stuff on sale. This is one of the greatest traps in our financial lives, and yet we all do it. Look around your household and in your closet. How many things did you purchase not because you needed them, but because they were on sale?

Sales are one of the leading causes of debt. We build debt based on things we don't actually need, but buy anyway because we think we are getting a good deal.

When we find ourselves perusing the sales rack, we think we have a saving mindset. We believe that we are saving money by buying items from the sale or clearance section. We get in a sale frenzy and start talking about all the money we are saving!

When I bought the dress for $50, I thought I saved $150, but I actually spent $50! It is still spending, no matter if it was on sale or not. In other words, our saving mindset is actually a spending mindset when it comes to sales. Whenever we shop for things that are not necessary, our spending mindset is activated, even if we save 99% on the price.

However, if you do need to go to the store, be aware of the items surrounding you. When you see something you want or like, ask yourself, "Do I truly need this?" or, "How often would I use this?"

Even if it only costs a few dollars, these things add up! Five dollars here, ten dollars there can add up to hundreds of dollars over the year. Before you purchase anything, make sure it is something you need or will use a lot. If you are in debt and trying to get out, spending on anything but essentials will just dig your financial hole even deeper.

"It was an emergency, I am sad/mad/feel needy."

I had a friend growing up who absolutely loved to shop. Her parents would give her money quite frequently, and she would spend every penny of it.

One day, she broke up with her boyfriend of a year. She stormed into my bedroom with a few bags of clothes from the nearest Nordstrom.

Shocked, I asked her, "Where did these clothes come from? Why did you buy these?" With a look on her face that told me she was taken aback, she exclaimed, "Me and Derek just broke up. I had to buy new outfits since I'm going back on the dating scene. It was an emergency!"

How many times have you had a bad day at work and reached for some extra quarters to buy a candy bar? Your bad day at work was an emergency for chocolate! You need to fill that void, right? No, not right.

If you bought a brand new computer and it crapped out on you a few months later, that would be an emergency. It was a totally unexpected event. If you got in a car accident and had medical bills, that would also be an emergency. Any necessary but unexpected expense is an emergency.

But emotional swings are not enough of an emergency to go out and buy a new wardrobe and get yourself off your financial track.

"If I had more money…"

A woman named Sharon Tirabassi was on welfare and struggling to make it as a single mother. Luck suddenly struck her one day and she found herself cashing in a check for $10 million. She'd won the lottery. Over the years, she spent this money on a fancy house, a new car, designer clothes, expensive trips, and handouts to family and friends.

Less than ten years went by and she was back riding the bus, working, and living in a rented house she couldn't call hers. She and her six children benefited from this lottery money, but then spent it all.

This is maybe the most-heard money myth today. Everyone says that if they had more money, they would be happy, they could afford their house, they could take their family on vacations, and they wouldn't have to work so hard.

If you cannot manage the money you currently have, you won't be able to effectively manage more money. More money is not the solution. If you make more, you will spend more if you have no discipline.

You have to know how to use your finances effectively so that you are not finding yourself in debt. If you cannot keep $1000 from blowing in the wind, what is going to make $10,000 stay? Sharon's story above is the perfect example of how more money won't fix a bad financial mindset.

Thankfully, you won't end up doing what Sharon did. How do I know this? Because you are willing to learn. You purchasing my book is proof of that. I will provide you with the best easy-to-follow tips to help you keep your money. You can also turn to Google and look up what you don't know. Lack of knowledge is not a good excuse these days. All the information you wish to know is so accessible. You do not need to be the Wolf of Wall Street to keep yourself on good financial terms. If you manage your money well, you don't need to fear you'll run out of it.

"I deserve it."

A woman named Liza fell on hard times. Her husband pulled money out of their retirement fund and blew the equity of their home on buying a bigger fishing boat. He said he deserved it. He went on a fishing trip one day and never came back. Liza had to turn her life around and start working when she used to be a stay-at-home mom. There is no doubt that she was a hard worker and got dealt the short end of the stick in life, but when she found herself suddenly making a lot less money than what she was used to, she found herself in debt. Even though she was working and making money, she didn't know how to manage it. She didn't know where her new spending boundaries lay, so she often overspent her budget on nonessential stuff like getting her hair done or eating out too often.

Liza would complain about being in debt because she said that she deserved to make more money. She deserved to not have to worry about finances after being so royally screwed. It is true; she didn't deserve to be left bankrupt and alone by her husband.

But when it comes to finances, it is often not about what we deserve, but rather what we can or should afford. Most often, these concepts are not proportional. We often deserve much more than we can afford. Before material deserving, however, you should consider positioning your mental peace. Do you deserve the anxiety and stress coming from mismanaged money?

Even if you are the hardest-working person and you deserve some indulgences here and there, do you really need to buy that fifth purse? The financial choices we make because we feel like we deserve new items are what get us deeper into debt.

Everyone should treat themselves. Don't go through life not treating yourself. Life is too short. But what is the better treat in your situation? Is it a new Xbox, or is it finding yourself debt-free?

Getting yourself out of debt and accumulating healthy savings will help you gain peace of mind. The small amount of satisfaction you experience when you buy that new game is not going to last.

In fact, you are most likely going to feel even worse after you walk away from the store with the bag in your hand.

You deserve to be debt-free. Before you buy something else, think about *whether or not it is essential and if it is going to get you further into debt*. If it is not essential and just worsens your financial situation, skip purchasing it.

"I don't make enough money to save."

Let me tell you a little bit about my own personal story. I lived on $100-$200 a month. You read that right. Two hundred dollars at best! That is close enough to nothing. But even as I lived on so little a month, I still put aside some money to save.

How did I do this? I lived in a cheap student hostel so I would not have to spend extra cash on expensive apartments. I worked constantly, even during high school, giving supplementary classes in hopes of changing my situation, introducing new streams of income with each student who joined my class. I bought the bare minimum when shopping. I lived on cheap bread and salami with water. I didn't buy sodas or coffees; I only bought what was necessary.

Even though this is an extreme situation, I had to live through it to get to where I am today. And the most important point to be made here is that even with nothing, I still saved money. I put aside some of my income to feel safer. And I'm not talking about a lot of money here, sometimes only $5. But it was essential to my peace of mind to know that I had a tiny amount of money left in case I didn't get my wages the day I expected them. My grandmother used to say that the man who makes 100 forints (Hungarian currency) and spends 99 will always sleep tight. But the man who makes 100 forints and spends 101 will always be in trouble. Simple wisdom, yet it's true.

If you don't make a lot of money, there are still ways to save. Do you have a budget? If not, I will help you create one. So many people are in disbelief over where their money goes. Try anything you can to save some money so you can put away extra cash into savings. Stop buying expensive coffee. You can get a pack of coffee at Safeway at as little as four or five bucks. This pack will last you up to two months. Is it bad coffee? It is. I'm not going to lie. But one can't have champagne tastes on a beer budget. Unfortunately. I know this more than anyone. I'm sorry I can't say something more encouraging. I won't sell lies. Until you make more money and get out of debt, you need to cut your expenses. There is no easy way around it.

Hey, on the bright side, I assure you that with focus and dedication, you can turn that sinking financial ship around. I fixed my finances, got out of debt, and have accumulated more savings than my entire family in less than four years. How did I do it? Making the changes explained in this book.

Some quick saving tips, if you think you don't know from where to cut any more: Buy items in bulk to save money. My mom used to buy all our staple foods when she got her pension at the beginning of the month. Milk, oil, butter, bread, some cheap meat... all in bulk deals and into the cart, then into the freezer. They weren't Michelin-star meals, but you know... I still grew pretty tall.

Do you have credit card debt? Don't pay them off late. It's a way of saving money if you don't waste it on fictional yet real and useless expenses such as credit card debt. Pay credit card debt first. You must pay off your credit card debt anyway. Better do it with the smallest possible cost.

Write down every expense that you have in a month-long period. Everything, even down to the last toilet paper roll. At the end of the month, go through your household and find the items you didn't necessarily need.

Look over your list and see where you can cut out some expenses. Maybe go down on your cable package or switch cell phone companies. Any way you can save money, do it. When you find the amount of money you didn't need to spend in the month, put that number as your target savings for the next month.

My richest friend once told me that it is bollocks that rich people get rich by choosing the cheaper parking lot and coffee. They get rich by saving on big expenses, not switching their phones or their car frequently. While he is right that saving on big expenses will keep more money in your pockets, I find it highly untrue that small stuff doesn't add up. They do. Especially if one only has a small amount to play with. If someone has $100-$200 to spend a month, one Starbucks coffee's price can actually cover two days' worth of food. Not fancy food, but food nevertheless.

"We can beat the market, invest with us."

Are you familiar with the movie *The Wolf of Wall Street*? An ambitious and money-hungry stock broker, Jordan Belford, convinces a lot of gullible Americans to invest in various funds and stocks with the promise of miraculous returns. But Belford can't give a guarantee on how the market will behave. No one can. The experts of the experts who have access to computer programs that can make multiple thousands of exchanges per second… they can't predict market behavior with certainty. How, then, could some self-proclaimed expert or sensationalist media site do it? Let's just be clear here, if you read somewhere which funds to invest in, the best time to do it probably already passed. By the time the news made it to the internet, people who day trade for a living already knew about it and took advantage of it. This doesn't mean that you can't reap more humble benefits. You might. But it's not sure.

Here is some data for you. An astonishing 96% of actively managed mutual funds (actively managed meaning an expert constantly trying to optimize your portfolio to maximize profit—and commission) fail to beat the market over a long period of time.[v] 96%! That's ninety-six percent. A blind monkey hired to throw darts into a target would do better than that. And this is not to diminish the knowledge of brokers, it's to show how unpredictable the market, in fact, is. More on this topic in the chapter for investments.

Realize that all of these money myths are just that—they are myths! You don't need to believe them or buy into their lies. These myths are not healthy or helpful and will only harm your future wealth. In the next chapter, we will discuss the psychology of spending, "how they get us," and how to release ourselves from the grips of compulsive spending.

Chapter 3: Spending Plan

Now that we have taken a close look at the most common myths related to money, we can see how much depends on what we are spending our money on. To have more money in your pocket you can either make more or spend less. It's as simple—and hard—as that.

The Iowa Gambling Test

This research project was designed by researchers at the University of Iowa to simulate real-life decision-making. The participants had been shown four decks of cards. They were told that choosing some cards would win them money and some other cards would lose them money. The aim of the picking was to collect as much money as possible. They didn't know that the first two decks were "bad decks" and would lead to long-term losses and that the other two decks were "good decks" which would lead to long-term gains.

Their physiological measurements were registered while they made their choices. The data measurement showed that the participants realized the winning or losing quality of the decks after choosing about forty to fifty cards. They could explain why picking cards from the last two decks was a better idea. But the participants had another mental process measured apart from the previous one.

The participants showed stress responses (higher skin conductivity, more sweat in their palms) after picking only ten cards from the "bad decks." Subconsciously, they foresaw the punishment followed by the bad pick thirty or forty cards before they could logically explain it. Shortly, their subconscious mind figured out the game long before their conscious one.

The human mind doesn't work on rational deliberation only. It is a mish-mash of emotional and rational decisions. Emotional responses usually are automatic and heuristic-based fueled by intuition. Intuitive responses come naturally and quickly even if there is not enough information to comprehensively jump to a conclusion. These types of decisions are subconsciously made. The vocal manifestation is preceded by biological ones such as sweating, increased heartbeat, skin conductivity, and others.

Rational answers, opposed to emotional ones, are conscious. However, they are slow and require effort. Logical and rational responses are much harder to make, and therefore many people automatically rely on their intuitive gut answers in most cases.

When it comes to spending, buyers are more inclined to take out their credit cards led by emotional processing. They make a decision based on how they feel about the product, not on whether or not the object in question is needed or worth the price.

Emotions vs. Rationality

When we buy something due to smart rationalizing we think that our decision is well founded. We imagine ourselves with all the perceived benefits the object of our desire will give us. We like to fantasize about our gains and benefits followed by the purchase. Sellers know this, and they specialize on stroking our ego with "just what we need" to make a sudden, emotional-decision–based purchase. Have you ever found yourself being turned on to consider a product essential even if ten minutes before you didn't even know it existed? For me, this product was a noise-cancelling headphone. One day I came across an advertisement about it. They promised locking out the outside world, peace and quiet on airplanes, great for doing yoga and meditation—all that I missed in life compressed in this device. It's great, it's useful, and it is $350. But that's a small price to pay if I'm concerned for my mental wellbeing, right? Right. Take my money, Mr. Bose.

To be fair, the money I spent on those noise-cancelling headphones was some of the best spent. I use the device almost daily. For sure it was an invaluable ally on flights, and we did lots of meditation sessions together. There are so many deterring examples of impulse purchases, though, for every good one. Branded jumpsuits, a new phone just out of boredom, a second leather jacket with decorations, a Lululemon yoga mat vs. one from Target, the 100th shade of lipstick (or the 99th, 98th… basically all after the 3rd), a MacBook Pro with all the perks vs. a standard MacBook Air… I could go on.

Marketers are careful to emphasize all the benefits you will get if you buy their product. They use words such as the best, the only, a product for smart, conscious, stylish people only and so on. You feel somewhat obliged to buy that product; otherwise you are not smart, conscious, and stylish.

The ace in marketers' decks is, however, not a future benefit, but the promise that the product will offer a quick and easy solution to our present pain. Why is that more effective? Because it is much easier to reenact our pain than to imagine future gains. Pain is real. Future happiness is not. Stating that someone will no longer suffer is a powerful motivator. Once we have the conviction that the seller understands our problems and can fix them, we'll be more likely to make the purchase.

The Traps of Social Influence

Influence: The Psychology of Persuasion by Robert Cialdini is a must-read on my shelf. It helped me learn how I should present myself on the market, but more importantly, taught me how to protect myself from the marketing influence of others. He has been researching and studying why and how people get influenced for more than thirty years. During this time, Dr. Cialdini securely concluded that in most cases people don't understand the factors that affect their behavior.

Below, I will summarize the six persuasion principles presented by Robert Cialdini that are usually used to influence buyers. I'll approach them from the buyer's perspective— as a warning; how to become a more aware consumer by recalling these principles and questioning your purchases based on them.

The Reciprocity Principle

When we get something, we almost feel obliged to pay back what we received. When someone gives you a compliment, you immediately start scanning that person to see what you can say in return, right? The reciprocity principle also explains why free gifts are so effective.

To make you feel indebted, sellers don't even have to give an expensive gift. It can just be some information or a small piece of a larger product that you'll be tempted to buy. The secret is that sellers give you something for free to first buy your good will and trust.

The Social Proof

This principle lays on the tendency of trusting more what's popular, or endorsed by our fellow humans, than those things that are not. For example, we are more prone to laugh when other people laugh in comedy shows, or more likely to buy when a satisfied customer tells her story with the product on *Top Shop*. We are more inclined to buy cooking equipment that is recommended by Gordon Ramsey or a friendly grandmother than one with zero endorsement. If we shop online, we tend to buy stuff that has more customer reviews and a rating of at least four stars instead of buying something with no reviews.

Commitment and Consistency

The best new customer is an old customer, says the golden truth of marketing. It's much easier to persuade an existing customer to buy another product from a store where they've purchased before, and were satisfied, than to bring a new customer in. This is why sellers have a specific strategy of how to keep people hooked to their store after their first purchase. And we, as buyers, are also happy to get that 30% coupon from the supplier we trust.

Sellers first earn customer loyalty, and then they make them commit to their product using different strategies. Customers feel automatically drawn to stick with them.

Customers are rewarded for their loyalty, with things like annual gifts or a higher discount percentage after spending a certain amount in that store. They feel that it's a good deal to stick with that vendor.

The Liking Principle

People are more likely to listen to someone they like, admire, or look up to when it comes to product recommendations. They are also keen to listen to the advice of attractive people rather than average ones, listen to people who are similar to them, and to those who are kind to them.

If a seller compliments something about me, I'm more inclined to buy something additional in that store or leave a tip. Or both. I almost feel obliged to—see the reciprocity principle. A free compliment for my money.

My boyfriend just bought a Dutch oven because his brother recommended it. You need to know that my boyfriend is a guy who doesn't buy even a mobile charger before he's spent one hour on Reddit researching it to make an informed decision about what he's allowing in his life. Yet he bought this two-hundred-something-dollar cooking pot just because his brother said so. That's the power of the liking principle.

Put your hand on your heart and be honest with yourself. How many times have you bought something just because your favorite star, your best friend, or your brother said so? Right?

Authority

People are attracted to authority and they respect it. They are open to follow the lead of experts, geniuses, and high achievers. A professor, an expensive suit, or a posh apartment sometimes is enough to convince the unsuspecting customer about expertise.

Headlines like "studies show," "experts proved," and "scientists say" are catchy, attractive, and trustworthy. People like to read or gain knowledge from people who seem to know what they are doing.

People are very insecure and uncertain when it comes to decisions they have to make without having any knowledge or emotional memory about it. They eagerly look outside themselves for information and professional guidance to validate their decisions. This is why authority figures have incredible influence on people who seek advice in their field of expertise.

Scarcity

People are genuinely attracted to unique or rare items because purchasing and owning these items makes them feel unique and special, too. In classic economic theory, scarcity relates to supply and demand. Namely, the higher the demand for an item, the more expensive it will get. Why? Because there are few items to purchase and a lot of people who compete to buy them; they are willing to pay a higher price for this product.

In other words, the less there is of something, the more valuable it seems. The more rare a thing is, the more people want it.

In most cases there is no real scarcity, just sellers making us believe it. Once, I bought a ticket to San Francisco. It had a reasonable cost and it had a little red label, informing me that there were only three free seats on that plane. I bought the ticket instantly, but curiosity led me back to the airline's page. Guess what? There were still three seats available even after I bought one. There were three seats available a week later, and a day before departure. Good game.

What is Compulsive Spending?

Have you ever watched the movie *Confessions of a Shopaholic*? It is a sweet, better-than-it-looks rom-com about a young journalist who is addicted to shopping. She is trapped in the maze of credit cards, collecting a debt of more than $16,000. She lives in constant terror of debt collectors, she even doesn't pay her rent for a few months, but she still can't stop shopping.

In the movie, it is not mentioned, but she has a compulsive buying disorder (CBD. No, not that CBD. Another type.), or oniomania. In practice this means that a person has obsessive shopping habits that bring adverse consequences upon them. Psychologists Kellett and Bolton defined it as "an irresistible, uncontrollable urge, resulting in excessive, expensive, and time-consuming retail activity [that is] typically prompted by negative affectivity" and results in "gross social, personal and/or financial difficulties." — (Kellett S., Bolton J. V. (2009). "Compulsive buying: A cognitive-behavioural model." Clinical Psychology and Psychotherapy.)

Compulsive buying disorder can be triggered by perfectionism, the desire of perceived acceptance by others, the need for control, or general impulsiveness. However, it can also be a manifestation of identity searching, social-position–gaining hopes, anxiety, low self-confidence, or depression. These reasons do not apply to all cases. Not everybody who experiences CBD suffers from depression.

For those who are wealthy, CBD might just seem like an everyday pastime. In many cases it really is. But for those who have a tight budget, this condition can produce disastrous results.

The difference between CBD and regular shopping is the compulsive, overwhelming desire to buy and spend against better judgment and the known negative consequences. Nonaddicted buyers buy for the sake of real need and utility, while compulsive buyers buy for mood improvement and balancing emotions. People suffering from CBD think just as intensely and as often about shopping as an alcoholic about the next drink.

People with CBD have a more complex problem than "retail therapy." As I said before, compulsive buying serves the temporary enhancement of emotional-need satisfaction. This emotion-regulation strategy swings between apprehension or anxiety to a temporary feeling of frenzy and positive excitement during the research and purchase of something. The compulsive buying cycle usually culminates in guilt or remorse, when the realization of how much money one spent on usually useless items overshadows the positive clouds, and bitter regret falls on them. The regret soon transforms into anxiety. And how do they end up soothing their anxiety? Yes, at the next shop. The cycle starts over again.

The answer to the question "*Is compulsive buying a mental health issue?*" is no. Compulsive spending behavior itself is not a diagnosable mental health condition. It's more a symptom of other psychological issues, like an insufficient sense of self-worth or addiction. According to some researchers, CBD is a form of obsessive-compulsive disorder. Others consider it something akin to an impulse control problem where the person seeks short-term gratification while ignoring long-term consequences.

Compulsive spending in most cases results in compulsive hoarding. People who give such great value to inanimate objects have the tendency to feel cumulated satisfaction with the more they have. Hoarding items can also give a false sense of security—I'm closely affected by this problem. This leads, however, to another issue. On one hand, the more things hoarders own, the more secure they feel. On the other, the more they have, the more terrified they become of losing it all.

How to Overcome Compulsive Buying

To overcome compulsive buying we need to raise awareness about our problem. The best way is to work with a licensed therapist. An objective, unbiased third party can help us with healthy emotion-regulation strategies to understand where our compulsive buying tendencies come from, and overcome the urge of mindless buying in the future. The therapist can help identify the causes and negative consequences of our actions, and help us figure out healthier ways of coping.

There are no specific therapies designed solely to overcome compulsive shopping habits, but there are many forms of therapy that can help people address this issue. Two therapies produce outstanding positive results: cognitive behavioral therapy and therapies using different mindfulness techniques. The former proves to be the best when used in groups. Two psychologists, Michel Lejoyeux and Aviv Weinstein, conducted research about the efficacy of cognitive behavioral therapy in case of CBD. They highlighted that a proper psychiatric evaluation should precede the therapy to find the most appropriate recovery program for the patient. If the patient receives the most fitting therapy, it will decrease their compulsive buying tendencies after only ten weeks of participation. The latter, the mindfulness technique therapies, resulted in impulse improvement, better emotion management, and self-acceptance.

People with compulsive buying tendencies might want to add financial counseling to their therapy. Anything can be useful, from self-help books to online finance and budgeting courses to group counseling meetings. Raising awareness about unhealthy shopping habits can improve a lot about our finances.

If you feel that you suffer from a milder, or more severe, version of CBD, you might want to consult a counselor. From a budgeting point of view it is critical to keep your shopping impulses under control. Otherwise, even if you manage to budget and save in the short term, you won't be able to keep it in the long term.

A little nugget to remember the next time you're about to embark on a shopping spree. Because of the nature of the US tax system, the cost of purchasing is actually higher than it looks like. Let's say you find a pair of pants for $75. Assuming you're in the 25% tax bracket, the actual amount you'd need to earn to buy these pants is $100. That's because $100 taxed at 25% is $75.[vi]

Stories on Frugality

If you're familiar with the book *The Millionaire Next Door* by Thomas J. Stanley and William D. Danko, you may have read that millionaires by and large don't look and act as we'd expect. When we imagine a person with millions to spend, we usually picture someone wearing luxury brand stuff, driving a Ferrari, and pushing through crowds flashing a handful of Ben Franklins demanding to be assisted first as they are a million-aire. You don't imagine them like this? Okay, maybe it's just me.

Surprisingly, chances are high that the cash-flashing, Gucci-wearing schmuck is far from being a millionaire. Data shows that these hyper-consuming people have high income but low net worth. They are the part of the population who help out actual millionaires. How? For example, by leasing new cars. Most millionaires wouldn't do that. Thomas Stanley's research showed that out of the hundreds of millionaires he interviewed, 80% never leased a car. Not even a scooter. They usually buy the barely used cars of the cash-flashers who can't afford their lease payments after an economic meltdown.

This is exactly what Ken, a multimillionaire in his fifties, did. But not only this. He and his family have lived in the same house for 25 years. And yes, he has the same wife. The biggest wealth-eaters in America are largely frequent moves and divorces.

Ken was lucky to see a great example on how to manage finances. His father was a surgeon who left behind an estate worth over $10 million when he passed away. Ken shared his family's success in accumulating wealth.

"My dad was frugal. We never knew he was wealthy until we received an accounting statement for his estate. We were shocked. He used to buy a new car, a Buick, about every eight years. That's when the wheels would likely fall off! I get a tremendous amount of satisfaction from saving and investing... that's what Dad did. Like father, like son. I am frugal; my wife is even more frugal. I buy my cars used from small-size leasing companies, often undercapitalized, that take back vehicles from lessees who can't make the payments. I recently bought a car for $22,000... a year and a half old. It listed for $35,000. The leasing company had four of the same model. I just call the leasing companies listed in the Yellow Pages."[vii]

Stanley and Danko shared the seven things that people who accumulate a substantial amount of wealth do.

1. They live below their means.

2. They allocate their time, energy, and money efficiently, in ways conductive to building wealth.

3. They believe that financial independence is more important than displaying high social status.

4. Their parents did not provide economics outpatient care.

5. Their adult children are economically self-sufficient.

6. They are proficient in targeting market opportunities.

7. They chose the right occupation.[viii]

Here are some other fun facts about millionaires:

- About two-thirds of working millionaires are self-employed. While self-employed people only make up less than 20% of the American working population, about two-thirds of them are millionaires.

- About 80% of millionaires in Stanley's research are first-generation affluent.
- They live on less than 7% of their wealth, on average. Well below their means.
- On average, they invest nearly 20% of their household's realized annual income.[ix]

Wealthy and having a high paycheck mean different things. You can make half a million a year and not be considered wealthy. Net worth is defined as the current value of one's assets less liabilities. There is a strong connection between a person's income and age and how much this person should have as net worth.

Stanley and Danko suggest an equation on how to determine how much your net worth should be if you used your money smartly. "Multiply your age times your realized pretax annual household income from all sources except inheritances. Divide by ten. This, less any inherited wealth, is what your net worth should be."[x]

So, let's say I'm 29 years old and my income is $50,000 a year (I made up this number). I would multiply this number by 29 and then would divide it by ten. According to this calculation, my net worth should be $145,000.

What is your number? Does your net worth fall in accordance with your income and age?

If it doesn't, you're not alone. So many people don't have a net worth they should have due to a million reasons. I, for example, often think and ruminate about what ifs surrounding my childhood. What if my mom didn't get sick and she could have taught me a responsible financial blueprint that I could have followed from an early age? What if my dad wouldn't have been a notorious spender and hoarder? What if I was born in the US, able to take advantage of so many great financial tools that are unavailable to anyone else? What if, what if…?

What if I taught myself everything that I failed to learn at home? What if I found the best financial instruments I can use and started using them *today*? What if I focused on myself, competed with myself, and set up financial goals for myself? What if you did the same?

Because, my dear reader, at the end of the day, it doesn't matter why we didn't make better financial decisions in the past. It doesn't matter we didn't have a good role model at home, that we come from a poor family, that school didn't prepare us. What matters is, what are we going to do now? There is a lot of good information on where to start in this book, in other books, blogs, forums—we can't have the excuse that we don't know. We only choose to not know.

So, why waste more time? Let's dig into your spending habits.

What do you spend on the most? You should know, take out your spending sheet. How much does it take to maintain your current lifestyle? In other words, how much do you spend in one month? Would you like to save (more) money?

Can you make more money to fatten your savings account? If the answer here is no, you first need to curb your spending. Saving money doesn't come easy for most of us. Especially when we live paycheck to paycheck, it seems like an impossible mission to put aside 10 or even five percent of our income. But here is the deal, you probably can save, you only need to reevaluate and re-prioritize your spending.

Your first task will be to:

Keep track of your spending over the next month.

Each day. Every item you pay money for. You may be surprised. "I just collected my monthly expenses, haven't I?" Yes, you did. You did add up an estimate. But in my experience—and of many other people—our retrospective estimates are often inaccurate. You didn't quite remember every bubble gum, soda, or snack you bought when you stopped at the gas station, did you? Not infrequently, $50-$100 or even more money can suddenly "appear" on the spending radar, things we didn't think about before. If you invested that $50 each month over a 20-year period with a 10% growth rate, it would become around $37,800. Not bad for chips and soda.

So please, jot everything down. Every little parking ticket. Do this for one month.

We tend to treat large lump sums of money differently than small amounts. We usually handle larger amounts in a more thoughtful way. What if we handled smaller amounts of money more carefully as well? I hope that after my example you'll see that even small amounts can have an impact in the long run.

I don't blame you if you treat a $10,000 bonus differently than a $10 happy hour cocktail. Spending $10,000 on cocktails would feel wrong, or bad, or crazy, right? Spending 10 bucks on that margarita? Not so much. Plus, it would be so painful not to drink the margarita for $10 when you're out with your friends. It would require serious delayed gratification. "No, Amanda, I will save this $10 on the margarita to invest it into my no-load, low-cost ETF portfolio." I think Amanda would be so shocked she'd stop drinking. Besides, it is hard to conceptualize the power of compounding interest on $10. Who would think that $10 could compound into $1,174 in fifty years without doing anything with it but having a 10% interest rate? If you put your pocket money on the stock market when you were ten and forgot about it, now you'd have more than a thousand dollars from it. It's not a lot of money, but again, we're speaking ten forgotten bucks here. Make the same calculation with $1000. Or better yet, just to shock you a bit... Say your great-great-great-grandfather left $10 on the stock market "unattended" with a 10% interest rate. The money grew there for 200 years. Those 10 dollars today would be worth... are you ready? $1,899,052,765. That's correct. Almost two billion dollars. If you ever questioned what the power behind "old money" is, there's a one-word answer: compounding. This calculation uses a lot of simplifications and a more optimistic stock market performance, but my point is still valid. Compounding is powerful.

Would you be more willing to save that $10 now? Would you consider more how to handle small amounts of money? How bite-sized daily choices could improve your financial life over the long run?

Okay, back to collecting your expenses. They are not linear, of course. You have a set amount of daily expenses, but then there are one-time larger expenses like buying a new computer because the old one broke. Or paying your tuition for a course. Or your yearly holiday. For these expenses, come up with a monthly estimate. For example, your tuition fee is $12,000. Divide this by 12 to find out how much the tuition costs you monthly: $1000.

After you've tracked your spending for a month, what do you see? Would you be able to save a couple hundred dollars monthly if you organized house parties instead of eating out with friends? Could you chop how much you spend on clothes in half? What do you actually need? And what do you need more—more nights out, or financial peace of mind? If the former is more important, there's nothing wrong with it. You're free to choose your priorities. But then don't be surprised about living paycheck to paycheck.

You don't have to deep-cut and bleed out to save money. There are creative and cheap alternatives to any activity. Are you social? Go out only once a month and organize the other get-togethers at someone's house where everybody brings something to eat and drink. Do you like shopping? I kid you not, some of my favorite and most worn clothes I got in secondhand stores. There are great little deals in stores like that, and the entire process of shopping is an adventure. Do you like delicious food? Cook it at home.

My boyfriend and I have a special monthly date night where we dress up nicely and cook a "fancy meal" together and eat it on our balcony. Our fanciest meal was a lamb stew with roasted pear, walnuts and Gorgonzola cheese, and a nice bottle of Cabernet. I must highlight that this was an expensive homemade meal, considering that lamb chops are the high end of the meat price hierarchy. We ate until we dropped for about $80. We had a similar meal at a normal (not high-end) restaurant a couple months before—that's where we got the idea. We left the restaurant slightly hungry and we paid $230 for the very same meal. Taxes, tips, service fee... You name it. The funniest part of it was the wine. We really loved the wine we got at the restaurant. We saved the label on a wine-rating app called Vivino. If you love to remember a good wine, it's a great way to store it. The restaurant charged us $100 for that bottle. For our special date night we got the very same wine for $25 from the store.

My point is, there are always ways to save money. And I won't even start calculating how much that $75 saved on the wine would compound into in 200 years...

With these numbers in mind, go back to your list of monthly expenses and consider where you could cut back some. Start by sorting out the nonnegotiable, must-spend-on items like bills, mortgage, loan payments, insurance, basic food, etc. Got them all? Great! Now subtract the number of absolute necessities from your income. Hopefully, there is still some money left. Take a hard look at it. First, decide how much you'd like to save for your future financial goals. You made the calculation in the previous chapter how much you need to save monthly to reach your one-, five-, ten-, twenty-year–term goals. Do you have enough left to save and still have some money to spend on nonessentials? If yes, try to commit to putting the required amount of savings into your savings account. The best way to stick to this is to automate the specific amount you want to save; ask your employer to send X amount of your paycheck directly to your savings account. Out of sight, out of mind, as they say.

If you have less money left than your savings goals, it's clear that you need to adjust your goals a bit—either the deadline for them, or the quality of them. For example, what was a five-year goal might instead happen in eight to ten years. Or instead of aspiring to save $50,000 in five years, aspire to save $30,000. Adjust.

Just like with a strict diet, it's unsustainable to strip yourself from all joys of life in the long run. It's not realistic to live only on bare necessities and savings. Or at least, it's very, very hard. At one point you'll ask, what's the point of working so hard and saving anyway? My life is empty and miserable. You need to be mindful to not burn out and then burn all your savings in the form of desperation compensation. Make sure to spend at least 10 percent of your income on "fun" stuff. But be mindful of them too. If you spend smartly, you can get 30 percent worth of fun from only 10 percent of your income.

When you assess a "fun" expense, ask yourself, "How could I replace this activity/ expense in a creative way? What could I buy/do instead that would still deliver me joy but wouldn't cost so much?" When you've got your answer, just do it.

Chapter 4: Debt

Right now, I can tell you exactly what the mathematical formula for the Pythagorean theorem is. It's $a2 + b2 = c2$. That is how you find a bunch of different measurements for triangles.

Now let me ask you this: How many times have you used the Pythagorean theorem since you graduated your high school math class? I bet that you have used it less than five times—including helping your child with their homework. And yet, that formula was drilled into my mind day after day throughout math class. Why? Who knows! But you know what I didn't learn in class? Why I shouldn't be buying my tenth pair of Nikes or my hundredth shade of lipstick.

I didn't learn how to do my taxes, how to manage my money, what compound interest or debt is. School taught me none of the "real life" stuff.

School won't teach you real-life finances. You could buy the upsold product of some finance guru for thousands of dollars. They will teach you how to be rich at the age of fifty for a price that requires you to mortgage your home. There you might learn real-life finances. They tell you the best tips, but you may have little money left to take action on those tips. However, to simply learn to manage your money, you don't need to go to those lengths.

People hate talking about debt. Some people say do not ever get into debt, others say take a risk and go into debt for a larger profit. Who can you believe these days? I get it, maybe you are knee-deep in debt and want out. Maybe you are thinking of going into debt and looking for guidance. We all get there at some point in life.

But before we make that decision, we hear a small whisper in our ear telling us various items of advice. And guess what? Oftentimes, that advice sucks. I hate to say it, but that angel on your shoulder isn't all that smart. Turns out that small voice is really what we have learned in the past and merely believe to be good advice.

Growing up, I constantly heard my grandparents talk about money. Talking is a generous term; most times, it was arguing—loud arguing. Even though they had some money, there seemed to never be enough. It drilled into my mind that money is bad. Money is a necessary evil, and the only way you get enough of it is to lie and cheat yourself into becoming rich.

People of my age in the US were told the best way to live your life is to go to school, get a mediocre-paying job, invest in a 401k and a home, and retire when you are 65. Along this path, they would pick up debt from student loans and buy a home. But this was considered "good debt." This mindset is what has led to the modern debt epidemic. We pull out debt after debt because we think it's good, that it will help us. It is good to have "free money" and to satisfy wishes quickly. But it backfires bitterly.

If you are in debt, you aren't alone. In fact, corporations also go into debt. A few notable companies are Lehman Brothers, AIG, and General Motors. All of these companies went into debt because they handled their money poorly. Bad financial decisions and money mismanagement is quite frequently a problem among companies, too—not just individuals.

A Short History of Debt

The US has had financial problems for the past 100 years, and the roaring monster who is responsible for most of these financial problems is known as Mr. Debt.

Debt started accumulating in crazy numbers in the aftermath of World War II. After the war, the housing market boomed and FHA mortgages were newly available. The debt was wrapped up in a big box with a pretty bow and made to look like what every American household should be.

People were then scrambling to buy a house and pull out enough debt to secure the house. They called these loans "easy debt" to make them sound desirable and fancy. People loved it! Your average person started accumulating debt big time.

This led to the states printing more money without enough coverage, and this balloon of uncovered financial aid grew bigger and bigger until... POP! 2008 came and the recession hit.

While this is a main source of our financial crisis, personal debt dates back even farther than the wars. It even predates the existence of money, per se. In the ancient times when people didn't have enough goods to offer in exchange for other goods, they often offered their work for food and other necessities. This often resulted in self-inflicted slavery. The rudimentary form of debt was physically horrifying. Today, stress coming from debt leaves mental marks. The origin is still the same—people spending more than they can afford.

Where is all this debt coming from? Personal debt is every credit card balance that goes unpaid, every loan taken out, and anything else you spent creditors' money on.

Why do so many of us find ourselves in debt? The reality of finding ourselves in the financial crisis is that our monthly income is not enough to afford our lifestyle. You might be thinking to yourself, "But I don't live a luxurious lifestyle!" That's probably true.

However, even non-luxurious lifestyles can create debt. Debt happens whenever your spending exceeds your income.

The problem occurs because we spend money we do not have. On top of this, the creditors lend us money that they don't have, and then they charge us interest on this loan, expecting us to somehow come up with money that doesn't even exist. There is actually more debt in the world than there is money to cover it. Society at large is playing a giant game of musical chairs.

Around and around debt goes, trying to grab those money chairs. When the music finally stops, everyone sits down as quick as they can! But there's always one person left out. This person gets eaten alive by debts. Figuratively, of course.

Since there is not enough money to cover the debt, you can imagine that the interest is a nonexistent amount as well. Following this logic, there will always be people who won't be able to pay off their debt plus the interest. There is always a sum of debt that is unable to be paid off. It sounds crazy, right?

The debt crisis is partially due to the fact that people aren't being paid more. The buying power of our income is similar as it was in the 1980s. When someone gets a raise, it is just counterbalancing with inflation. And in fact, people are sometimes getting paid even less now than they were back in the 80s (once you adjust for inflation).

Think of it like this: In the 1980s, a copywriter made maybe $5 a day. Bread only cost $0.50 a loaf. Easy to afford! Now, this same copywriter makes $25 a day, but bread now costs $3.00 a loaf. Before, a copywriter could buy ten loaves of bread from a day's wage. Today, he can only buy eight.

When adjusted for inflation, the copywriter now makes less than the copywriter in the 80s because the costs of goods and living have gone up. Since the buying power of wages didn't increase, neither did economic growth, and finally, the bubble popped.

But even though the costs of goods and living have gone up, we should still be able to afford to live. So why do so many of us find ourselves armpit-deep in debt?

Because the choice of goods increased significantly. There are more options of what to buy today. We also have a new power called marketing that makes us believe that we need every new gadget and we need it now, otherwise we're lame, unfashionable, and so on. Most people, however, don't make nearly as much as they would need to in order to keep up with the trends. So what do they do?

Do they wear the same pair of jeans and use the same car for ten years...?

Nope. They engage in debt.

The most popular forms of debt are credit card debt, student loans, auto loans, mortgages, and home equity lines of credit. If you do not have any type of debt, keep up this good habit. But if you are like the average American, you have at least one of these types of debt.

None of these debts start out with bad intentions. You think to yourself that you need to go to school, you have to buy a car, you need groceries, you need a house, and come up with a ton of other reasons.

No one sets out to get themselves into debt. We have been warned about debt our whole lives, but we are also told that if we do not have a good credit score, we'll never be able to buy anything.

And how do you get a good credit score? Racking up debt and paying it off within the allotted time.

Sound backwards? It is! Think of credit cards. You use them to buy everything you need, like groceries and gas. You look at your statement at the end of the month and it's way more than you thought. It's easier to spend the money when you don't have to fish it out of your purse. And so those bills go unpaid.

Credit card debt is highest among people in their sixties and seventies, but student loans and auto loans are highest among people in their twenties and thirties. This shows that most people struggle with debt, but different debts plague different age groups.

It is easily noted that debt causes stress. You know when your friend pays for your lunch and you feel the immediate need to pay them back? That's how debt feels too! It causes everyone stress.

But some debt may be unavoidable in short-term circumstances. What do you think about debt? Do you think it is necessary to survive? Or do you avoid it? There may even be some things you feel like you could go into debt for.

What Would You Go Into Debt For?

Think of what matters to you. Think of what you want your successful life to look like. Now think of things you believe are worthy to go into debt for. Take a look at your financial goals and dreams. Which one would be worth going in debt for?

For example, if your top priority is family, you may be comfortable going into debt to get a mortgage to have your family in a safe and stable environment. If your dream is to become a professor, you may be comfortable pulling out student loans.

After you figure this out, check your list of everything you spend your money on. How much do these lists overlap? If you spend money on cable, getting your nails done, and going out to eat, but you only feel comfortable going into debt for student loans, those lists do not overlap at all.

Oftentimes, we find that our lists don't overlap much. This is because our brains are hard-wired to work in instant-gratification mode. When you reward yourself, your brain releases dopamine and you get excited. That's why you love to buy those new shoes or devour a piece of chocolate cake.

Our brains make us believe that we need these daily indulgences, when in reality, we don't! This short-term gratification doesn't lead to lasting happiness, but instead leads to more debt. Often, it's not even the debt we'd consider worth "dying" for.

No matter what your reasons are for going into debt, you have to be careful. Debt can sweep the rug out from under your feet before you can realize it. One day you're only $100 in debt, and the next, you wake up drowning in thousands of dollars of debt. Let me give you an illustrative example. Say you have $3,500 credit card debt with an interest rate of 17% and you're 30. You pay the minimum payment monthly to the issuer. How long will it take to pay off the debt? Any guesses? Let me tell you, 35 years. Above the original $3,500 you'll also pay $7,662 in interest. More than double of the original amount will be interest payments.[xi] Was it worth getting into debt for that $3,500 thing?

Every time you contemplate going into debt, you must think about whether or not it is worth it in the long run. To stay afloat, get out of debt, and live the life you want, you must have a good financial planning system in place. You have to resist the urge to buy today at tomorrow's expense.

Getting Out of Debt

I already mentioned that when I was a student, my income was around $200 a month. This was hard to live on, and when I found myself wanting a new computer, I decided to pull out a student loan for $1000. Even if I'd dedicated all of my monthly income to pay off this student loan, it would have taken me five whole months to pay off. But I was desperate, and my mind fixated on this computer.

Literally the day after I applied for the student loan, my uncle gave me a computer as a gift. I was overjoyed! But guess what I didn't do? I didn't return the $1000 student loan. Nope, instead, I spent every last penny. And did I spend it on good things? Not exactly.

I took that thousand dollars and bought new clothes, teeth whitening treatments, and Christmas gifts. The key takeaway here is never apply for a loan. But if you must, don't do it around the holidays. At the time, taking the student loan did not seem like a bad idea, but as soon as I started to pay it off, I regretted it bitterly. $1000 quickly became $1500, and I realized how stupid my choice was.

I had to learn my lesson the hard way. But at least I did. And let's face it, the amount could have been worse. For many, it is. I decided to set out to inform and teach others to not make the same mistakes. If you are not currently in debt, try to not get into it. Especially if you don't have a stable enough repayment plan.

If I could turn back time, I would never have applied for the student loan. Even for the computer, I would not have gotten it. Knowing what I know now, I would have saved my money and purchased that computer at a later time. I paid more than $500 to the bank due to interest. I got nothing on that money—no goods, no happiness, only the vague joy of buying useless stuff quicker than usual.

The best way to get out of debt quickly is to not wait. As soon as you can, start paying off any loan that you have. When you wait and the interest accumulates, it is much more difficult to pay it off.

Let's say you have a loan that you pay $100 toward every single month. When your monthly check comes in and you made $500, don't think that. Instead, think that you made $400 because you already know that $100 is going straight to the loan. This little psychological trick can help you stick to your budget. You do not have $500 a month to spend because that $100 is not yours. Recognize that whatever is paid to loans is not part of your income. You can't escape it. Death, taxes, and debt collectors will always find you.

The best course one can take to get a grip over their financial life is to pay debts off quickly, starting with the ones with the highest interest rates.

1. If you have savings, use it to get rid of your debt with the highest rate.

Why? Because the interest rate on debts of credit cards or car loans is higher than what you'd realistically receive on any investment. Where would you have a 15-20% interest rate in the investment world? Other than some very hazardous ventures, of course. Say you have $2,000 saved up in the bank for a 3% interest rate (which is a very generous one). Keeping this money in the bank for a year will make you $60. Having a loan of $2,000 with 15% interest will grow $300 bigger after the first year. You save $60 just to spend $300. That's a $240 loss. That's why financial experts advise that as long as you have high-interest debts, work on getting rid of those.

If you use your $2,000 savings to pay off your $2,000 loan, you won't earn any interest that year—but you also don't have to pay an additional $240 for the loan's interest. I'd call that a win.

2. Refinance where you can.

Refinancing is a process where you transfer your debt from a high-interest-rate loan to a lower-rate loan. It is much better to pay 7% and borrow money than to not borrow money and keep paying 17%. If you find yourself being crippled by your credit card debt, apply for a card with a low-interest rate and transfer your current debt to that.

When you move your money—and debt—to another bank, the new bank is willing to do this for you because they want your business, so they are going to give you a lower interest rate. You can shop around at different banks and companies to find the lowest interest rate available.

Try looking for one that keeps a low and steady interest rate throughout the debt. Some banks will have interest rates that rise after a few months or a year. When you do the balance transfer, always double-check the terms and conditions. You don't want to move your balance to another bank only to find that it is worse than the first one. The devil always lies in the fine print.

3. Pay on time like your life depends on it.

Your financial life certainly does. Not only because you can accumulate hefty late payment fees, but also because anyone from a future employer to a landlord can look at your credit history. If you give the impression of someone who doesn't pay on time, you may be quoted higher fees and interest rates on anything from regular loans to mortgages. If you have late payment history, there's not much you can do about that. But you can always improve your

FICO score by sticking to paying your debts on time.

It is important for you to have a good FICO credit score. The FICO score is "a credit score in the United States that represents the credit worthiness of a person, the likelihood that person will pay his or her debts." Many institutions will use this credit score to evaluate their risk when they lend you money. Banks and credit card companies will use this number to decide how much they can safely lend to you. A widespread use of credit scores has made credit easier to attain for many consumers.

The FICO score is the most widely used measurement for "repayment ability" and ranges from 300 to 850. If you have a credit score of 750 to 850, then the risk of lending to you is fairly low. This is considered an excellent score, and if you fall into this range, then you will have access to the lowest rates and best loan terms.

If you are wondering how you get your credit score, you're not alone. Data from your credit report gets put into five major categories that make up your FICO score. The scoring model applies different weights to different categories.

For example, 35% of your score is made up of your payment history and whether you always pay off your balance or if you are often late. 30% of your credit score is how much you owe on different loans or credit cards, 15% is comprised of how long your credit has been accumulating, 10% is made up of new credit, and the remaining 10% is affected by the types of credit cards you use. So as you can see, there are lots of different factors here. The most important is how you pay your bills. If you pay your bills and don't let them gather interest, you are more likely to have a better FICO score.

Credit-card-free through college.

If you are currently a college student, try to avoid credit cards. A college education does not guarantee that you are going to know how to manage your finances. With the sky-high prices of tuition these days, it is best to not get into more debt than you need to. That means avoiding those credit cards. You won't have a stable income (probably), so you can easily end up spending more than you can afford when it doesn't need to be paid off until the end of the month. That is how many people end up in debt way too early. School won't teach you how to use your credit card wisely, anyway.

It's better that you don't spend more than you can safely afford. Your credit score is important and can be detrimental to your future if you ruin it in your youth.

How to Choose a Good Credit Card

A good credit card means one that is best fitted to your needs. If you know you'll carry a balance from month to month, the most important aspect of your card should be to have a low interest rate, or in other words, as low an APR (annual percentage rate) as you can get.

If you tend to pay your balance in full each month and you're sure you can do this consistently, in your case the APR is not so important. In your case, the most important factor is to find a card with no annual fee and preferably one which offers a grace period—a little cushion of time the bank doesn't start charging you interest. Don't forget considering certain perks credit cards offer. If you travel often, choose a card which gives "reward points" for every dollar you spend.

If you have problems handling money or you have a bad credit history, it might be a good choice for you to pick a secured credit card or just a debit card.

Knowing your needs, you can check out some websites for the best credit card, like www.credit.com. You can also check out www.cardtrak.com or www.lowcard.com. You could try to get a low-rate card through a labor union or credit union if you are part of any. You can visit your local banks for better deals than the national average as well.[xii] But always, always read the fine print for hidden fees. Remember, if something sounds too good to be true, it is because you don't know the whole story.

How Can You Get Rid of Your Debt?

Stop creating more debt.

This one may seem obvious, but I still have to say it. The first step to getting rid of your debt is to stop creating more debt. Stop purchasing more stuff. Even if you have a few "extra" dollars in the bank, it doesn't mean you should purchase something else. Just because you might be able to buy it doesn't mean you should.

Lots of people have a hard time saying no. If you find yourself unable to stop purchasing things, reevaluate your goals. Ask yourself what makes you happy. Is it acquiring more things? I bet this does not give you a lot of happiness. If buying things does make you happy, it is short-term happiness. What will make you happier, more stuff or financial peace of mind?

Rank your debts.

The second step in getting out of debt is running inventory on your debts and then rank them in order of urgency. The debt with the highest interest rate is your most urgent one.

Go through your expenses.

In the previous chapter, I talked about writing down every expense for a month. Grab that paper again. Look at your expenses and rate them in order of importance and urgency. Your high-interest debt repayment should be the first one on your list. Go through the expenses and try to find any that you might be able to cut out.

For example, if you treat yourself on a weekly rib-eye steak, try cutting that out completely or only doing it once a month. Less important but pricier expenses are easy to cut out. Just think about how important your debt repayment is. If you don't pay your debt off in time, you can incur expensive fees, which add up quickly.

Schedule your repayment.

Getting out of debt is as easy as paying off what you owe. However, with a limited income, that can be hard. The loans seem to get bigger and bigger, and you can feel like you are at a loss on what to do. Once you decide what expenses you can cut out and how much money you can put toward your debt each month, map out how long it will take for you to pay off your debt.

For example, maybe you are able to pay $300 toward your debt every month. Let's say you have credit card debt of $500 and then a student loan of $1,000. You will put the $300 toward your credit card payment for two months until it is paid off because that's the highest interest rate. Once that is paid off, you roll over your payments into your student loan payment.

So for the next three months, you will pay the whole $300 to your student loan payment. Each time you pay off a debt, roll that money into paying off the next debt. When you are 100% debt-free, save that money each month to create a good savings or investment account.

Create multiple income streams.

If you ever talk to a successful and wealthy individual, they will tell you that you have to have multiple streams of income. Your nine-to-five job just won't cut it if you want to be financially free. The internet has created an abundance of opportunities for you to make some side cash.

This can be as easy as walking your neighbor's dogs, doing yardwork, or working completely online. You can learn the tricks and trades of penny stocks if you have some extra money, or you can work on freelance websites using skills that you already have.

Sites like Fiverr and Upwork are easy enough to sign up for and make money from in your spare time. If you have any skills like writing, you can find jobs writing on Upwork. You can become a personal assistant, cover designer, or even find freelance IT jobs. The options are almost unlimited. Where there is a will, there is a way. Becoming a freelancer (even if only part time) is an easy way to make money without investing your hard-earned income.

If you want to be successful on freelance sites, don't hesitate to put yourself out there. Apply for the jobs that excite you and challenge you. Not only will you get to learn something new, but it can create lasting relationships with clients who will use your service again.

Discussing Different Kinds of Loans

Student Loans

If you find yourself in trouble when paying back your student loans, you might be able to do something about it. Talk to your loan servicer and try to negotiate a repayment plan that fits your needs better.

First, you might need to find where your loans are (which may not be so obvious). Go to www.nslds.ed.gov to locate your loan. The National Student Loan Data System has access to track every federal loan.

If you have multiple loans under the same servicer, you can ask for unified billing (loan serialization in technical terms). While this step doesn't change anything about the amount you have to pay, it might help you become more organized and punctual with your payments.

You can also try to consolidate your loans. This means that all of your loans will be crumpled into one big chunk of loan with a new interest rate. This is a sensible step only if your loans were issued before July 1st, 2006. Check out www.loanconsolidation.ed.gov for further information.

When you choose the way to repay your student loans, keep in mind that the less you pay monthly, the longer it will take to repay all the loan—and the more interest you'll end up paying. There are three types of repayments:

- **Extended repayment:** This choice allows you to pay off what you owe over a longer period of time—between 12 to 30 years. As a rule of thumb, the length of time you'll be given to repay will be determined based on how much you owe.

- **Graduated repayment:** This type of repayment allows you to repay smaller amounts during the first couple years and then gradually increase your monthly repayment fee.

- **Income-based repayment:** This method helps you to not pay more than a certain percentage of your income. Naturally, the more you make, the more you'll have to pay—and vice versa. If you don't manage to pay your loans back in 25 years, the government will forgive the leftover debt. But you'll have to pay income tax for the "forgiven" amount the same year.[xiii] To learn more, go to www.ibrinfo.org.

Once your debt is fully paid off, commit to being financially responsible. You must change your financial attitude to avoid getting into debt again at all costs. When you get into debt, you find yourself in a well that is very hard to climb out of.

Private Loans

Private loans are not federal loans; usually, private banks issue them, and most importantly, very often they are much more costly for the borrowers. Their Achilles heel is that their interest rates are not capped. Their interest rate can go up to two or three times of those of federal loans.

Only touch private loans if you maxed out all federal loans and they are really a last resort.

Buy Used Cars

You'll be paying significantly less for a used car, thus, you will be much better off in repaying your car loan—if you are applying for one.

While used cars always have a bit of risk to them in terms of quality and hidden problems, you can minimize these risks. Ask the dealer about the car's inspection history and hire a private and independent mechanic to have a look at the car. If you buy the car from a private owner, check the car's vehicle identification number (VIN) at www.carfax.com. They have a detailed background check on vehicles.

Stay on Track with Your Credit Scores

You can get a free copy of your credit reports at www.annualcreditreports.com, and you can pay to get your credit score at www.myfico.com.

The first step to financial independence is to get out of debt and keep yourself out of it. Everything else comes after that.

Chapter 5: Banking Basics

I remember when I was a child, I often heard my grandmother saying, "You need to put your money in the CEC." CEC Bank is a state-owned Romanian banking institution, and my grandparents swore that this bank was the safest way to save money. My grandparents hated foreign banks, the stock market, and everything that was not owned by the state. The state, to them, who grew up and lived most of their life in the Cold War, represented safety.

People's lives in general revolved around their bank next door for a long time. They applied for a mortgage there, for their credit cards and debit card, and for their savings accounts. It was easily accessible and convenient.

Things are different today. Ever since we've had access to the internet and online banking, distances are at our fingertips, and we'd much rather get the best credit card deals than the closest ones. We might even keep our savings account in an online bank to get higher interest.

If you ask why we even need banks at this point… Although most banking tasks you can easily solve from the comfort of your home, there are two major needs that banks still satisfy the best. These are ATMs which supply us with cash, and a complex checking account. Our major goal selecting a bank and other financial services should be to maximize interest on savings, get the lowest fees, and do both as conveniently as possible. This chapter is dedicated to help you do just that.

Let's talk a little bit about the types of financial institutions you can choose from.

Regular Banks

Institutions under the government's agency can call themselves a bank, savings bank, or savings and loan (S&L). From a practical point of view, they are all the same for small users like us.

Almost every bank (savings bank or S&L) falls under the protection of the Federal Deposit Insurance Corporation (FDIC). This means that your money is covered by federal deposit insurance up to $250,000 per depositor per insured bank. Check out www.fdic.gov/deposit for more information on each bank.

Banks sometimes sell uninsured investment opportunities these days, so make sure that the type of account you're about to open is covered by federal deposit insurance.

Credit Unions

Credit unions are somewhat different than banks. They are run on nonprofit terms by people who have a shared interest, like a profession. The upside of credit unions is that they offer slightly lower rates on loans, pay higher interest on savings accounts, and generally charge less on everyday tasks than regular banks. Your money is federally insured in a credit union just as it is in a regular bank ($250,000 as of 2019).[xiv]

The downside of credit unions is that some are actually not FDIC insured. "The National Credit Union Insurance Fund (NCUSIF), which is backed by the U.S. Treasury, insures your funds. The National Credit Union Administration (NCUA), an agency of the U.S. government, administers NCUSIF coverage."[xv] Make sure to inquire if your union falls under the protection of the FDIC. You can check out this website to research this question yourself: https://mapping.ncua.gov/ResearchCreditUnion.aspx. The other drawback of credit unions is that there are not as many ATMs available to withdraw cash as regular banks have.

If you like the idea of these nonprofit "banks," you can check out if there is such a union in your area and if you could join it. Go to www.cuna.org, the Credit Union National Association's website, or give them a call at 800-356-9655 and inquire which unions you may be able to join.

Three Things to Look For When Choosing a Bank

- Free checking. Most banks offer this, but just to be sure, double-check this aspect of your existing account or the account you're about to open. The best option is a bank that allows you to write as many checks as you need and whatever amount you need.

- Easy access to ATMs and branch locations. This can save you some bucks as banks usually don't charge for cash withdrawal if you do it through their own ATMs. ATMs of other banks can charge up to $3 to withdraw. If you often withdraw cash, having an ATM or a branch of your bank nearby can prove very useful.

- Online and mobile banking. While some people feel more comfortable going into the bank and talking to a real human, there is little one can't do through an online bank account these days. You can also spare yourself from accumulated clutter by getting your statements online. Mobile banking gives you access to your bank accounts anywhere at any time. It simplifies life a lot to do most of our finances online.

What to Take into Consideration with Your Checking Account

- Check your balance fairly often. Sometimes there can be fraudulent transactions on your account, or even bank mistakes that you wouldn't notice otherwise, and it can cost you anywhere between a couple dollars to a couple thousand. It's useful to keep receipts from transactions until they become visible online so you have proof you can dispute with the bank.

- Double-check your overdraft protection plans. Banks can charge for bounced checks, sometimes even more than what you owe to the person you wrote the check for. This amount can be as high as $30.

Banks usually provide an overdraft protection program that you can enroll in and thus you'll be protected from these charges. But don't be thankful to them just yet, as this program often costs more to enroll in than the amount it is supposed to protect you from.

Basically, when you use your debit card, withdraw cash from an ATM, or write a check to someone with more than what you currently have in your account, the bank may let the transaction go through for a flat fee, which usually is somewhere between $30-$40. Also, some banks, in addition to the initial fee, might charge you for each day your balance is negative. This can be anywhere between $5-$15 per day. Thus, you can end up accumulating hundreds of dollars in fees for one overdraft transaction.

How can you get around this? You need to take initiative and tell your banker when you're opening your account that you explicitly don't want to be enrolled in the courtesy overdraft protection plan but to instead use the money in your savings account whenever you'll end up with a negative checking balance. While this is not a great solution either, usually you lose less money as the interest on the overdrawn amount can be as peppery as 18%. [xvi] In sum, the best overdrawn protection plan is to not spend more than what you have.

- Link your checking and savings accounts if you have them at the same bank. This way you can transfer money between them without any extra cost. You can add money to your checking account whenever you need it even through your mobile app. Some banks might charge you some fee for the transfers, but much less than any overdraft fee.

- Don't get bamboozled by interest-bearing checking accounts. They usually require you to keep a lot of money in your account but give a ridiculously small amount of interest. For example, you need to have $5,000 in your account all the time to get the 0.05% interest as a reward, which will be $2.5 after a year. If, however, your balance drops below $5,000, you may need to pay $20 in fees. Plus, considering that inflation is about 3%, this account won't shelter you from that either.

- Use direct deposits for your salary. You can ask your employer to send you your salary electronically directly to your checking account if you have regular income. You can ask your bank to waive their minimum balance requirements and reduce their service charges.

- When something doesn't seem right, call your bank. When you check your balance and you notice some penalty fee, make sure to call your bank and ask them why you got it. If you disagree with the fee, try to explain to them why it should be erased. If you're not a notorious "offender," there's a good chance that the fee can be waived.

What to Take into Consideration with Your Savings Account

Let's be real for a second. A bank's savings account is not an opportunity where you'll make your next million thanks to compounding interest. And it shouldn't be. The purpose of a savings account at a bank is to have an emergency fund in a safe environment. Your emergency fund should be somewhere between three to six months' worth of expenses. The money you keep here is liquid, meaning you can withdraw from it without any penalty.

You can have a savings account at the same bank where your checking account is—for money transferring between accounts, this could be quite useful. But you can also shop around to find the highest interest-paying savings account. Check out www.bankrate.com and www.bankingmyway.com to find the best deals on the market. Let's see what type of savings accounts are out there:

- **Regular savings accounts.** This is the typical savings account offered by banks with a negligible interest rate. Usually, a minimum balance of $300 to $500 has to be maintained. They are safe and liquid.

- **Money market accounts (MMAs).** You'll likely need up to $4,000 to open such an account. This type of savings account usually needs a higher minimum balance, somewhere around $1,000, and if your balance goes beneath this number you might need to pay a monthly account maintenance fee. MMAs are liquid just like regular savings accounts but they might pay a higher interest. While this certainly could sound good, the downside of MMAs is that they require you to tie down a larger amount of cash. Some internet-based banks can have some noteworthy MMA perks, so it's not a bad idea to investigate.

- **Internet-based savings accounts.** As such banks have very low operational costs (fewer employees, no physical location), they generally offer higher interest rates for savings than regular banks. (I must highlight that this is not set in stone and internet bank rates may change in the future.) Another upside of these bank accounts is that they require no minimum cash. Choose an internet bank which is federally insured. This way you'll be protected up to $250,000 just like with a regular bank.

- **Certificates of deposit (CDs).** These are savings products that pay you a fixed interest rate (usually) if you keep your money in them for a given period of time agreed in the CD's term. Their maturity varies between one to three months to up to ten years. In most cases, CDs have a better interest rate than regular savings accounts or MMAs. When you purchase a CD you make a one-time investment and earn interest until the term is complete. If you wish to put more money in CDs, open a new CD. The opening amount of CDs can vary but you usually need $500-$1500. CDs offer you a tradeoff where you tie down your money, compromising liquidity for higher returns. If you withdraw money from the CD before the term is complete, you'll face a hefty early withdrawal fee. You may lose all of your interest plus some of the starting capital. Think twice before you tie your money in CDs—make sure you won't need it.[xvii]

Another important note on CDs. When you put money in CDs, you will have a fixed interest rate during your term. So, for example, you bought a CD with a 5% interest rate with a two-year term. Let's say in a year the economy starts doing better and banks start to pay 6% interest on CDs. You're stuck with your 5% rate, as withdrawing money would mean higher fees than what one makes on the 1% interest difference—in most cases. It's better to either buy a new CD or wait until maturity and then reinvest your money in a new CD with a higher rate. If, on the other hand, the economy starts to do worse and interest rates drop to 3%, you'll still enjoy the benefits of a CD with 5% interest.

What to Take into Consideration When You Use ATMs

When ATMs became a thing, they were usually free to use—banks didn't charge any fees. They wanted to encourage people to use the machines instead of going to the bank for cash and keeping bank clerks busy with something that doesn't bring money to the bank. When people got properly used to ATMs, banks suddenly started charging fees, creating a billion-dollar business out of it. Many people end up paying hundreds of dollars in ATM fees in a year. Here are some tips to not feed the bank's belly.

- **Stick with your bank's ATMs.** They usually don't charge you for using their own ATM—or they charge you only after a certain amount of withdrawals. They will, however, charge you up to $3 or more if you use another bank's ATM. Find out what this fee is and assess your cash need accordingly.

- **Pay extra attention to surcharges.** It's not enough that your own bank will charge you for being unfaithful to its ATMs, the other bank will charge you a fee too, a so-called surcharge for using its ATM. Thus, you can end up paying $6 or more just to get your money in a physical form. Some places where people may need cash urgently, like casinos, malls, and airports may charge you an even heftier surcharge.

- **Stick to the essentials.** Try to avoid using ATMs for more than withdrawals and deposits. Banks might charge you for balance inquiries or transfers between accounts. Find out first whether or not your bank does that, and only then use more complex ATM services.

- You can be in a tricky situation if you don't have access to your bank's ATM.

Estimate how much cash you will need for the month and withdraw it in one setting—especially if you use an ATM other than your bank's. If you need to pay the surcharges and fees anyways, better do it only once.

- **Why not cash back?** Supermarkets and drug stores often give you the option to ask for cash back when you shop there. While the maximum amount of withdrawal is limited to $50-$60, it is usually fee-free. You end up better off than using a foreign ATM.

Chapter 6: Investing, the Path to Financial Freedom

What Is the Price of Freedom?

Financial freedom, more precisely.

The answer to this question is, it depends. It depends on your income, your average monthly expenses, and your savings' interest rates. The big-picture answer is very simple. If you spend 100% of your income—and more—you'll never be able to retire early. You'll be stuck in the rat race, living paycheck to paycheck.

If, let's pretend for argument's sake, you spend 0% of your income and you can sustain this after you retire, you can retire right now.

Most of us lie somewhere between these two extremes. Here we need to make some very important choices. Namely, how can we save a set amount of our income monthly? How can we save even more? You see, once you start saving your money, it starts earning interest. Money will make money. Then the interest on those earnings will earn even more money. Your financial life can quickly turn into an avalanche of exponential income. Once the money you make in interest exceeds your expenses, keeping in mind to leave enough gains invested to keep up with inflation, you're retirement ready. But here comes the capital BUT.

As we saw, savings accounts offer fairly humble returns; they rarely make up to inflation, even. The real snowball-effect triggers are investments.

We all know that stock markets are unpredictable and risky. They skyrocket one year and can tank the next. Volatility is just part of the deal. One thing is certain, regardless if the market goes up or down, no one knows where it will go next.

Investments simply have to make up a part of your financial freedom plan. Once you've paid off your debts and you have an emergency savings fund set up to cover three to six months' worth of expenses, it's time to check out how you invest safely. Believe it or not, there are safe investment opportunities out there fitting every level of risk tolerance.

Investing money can be very scary, and people are hesitant to take action without proper encouragement. So allow me to encourage you.

First, we need to finally establish how much money you can save each year. Use this link to see, with your current savings rate, how many years you have left until you reach financial freedom:

http://networthify.com/calculator/earlyretirement?income=50000&initialBalance=0&expenses=20000&annualPct=5&withdrawalRate=4

The website calculates with an annual return-on-investment rate of 5% (after discounting inflation) and an annual withdrawal rate of 4%. Greg has an annual income of $50,000. If he could have annual savings of $30,000, he could retire in 12.4 years. Use the calculator to insert your own numbers and see how many years you have left.

As you can see, the more money you can save up from your paycheck, the earlier you can retire. Also, the lower your expenses, the less you'll need to earn in interest to cover you month by month. Therefore, lowering your expenses can also aid you toward a faster retirement. It is very important to know where you stand right now financially, to take stock of where you are. If you didn't do the exercises in the previous chapter, this is your last chance to do it before we start discussing budgeting strategies in the next chapter. Believe it or not, more than half of Americans haven't ever tried to calculate how much money they need to retire. Why is that? The answer is simple, it's the same reason why so many don't want to step on a scale to see how much they weigh. They are too afraid to face the truth. It's a form of denial; trying to avoid making a change. You can't reach financial freedom unless you know how much it "costs."[xviii]

Let's go back for a minute to the example of Greg. Let's assume Greg can only save 10% of his income, namely, $5,000. Being able to save 10% of one's income is considered better than average these days. However, this number is still not amazing. If Greg only saves $5,000 annually, he can retire in 51 years. Take a look at the picture below:

Savings Rate (Percent)	Working Years Until Retirement
5	66
10	51
15	43
20	37
25	32
30	28
35	25
40	22
45	19
50	17
55	14.5
60	12.5
65	10.5
70	8.5
75	7
80	5.5
85	4
90	Under 3
95	Under 2
100	Zero

Picture 2: Savings rate—years-to-retire chart.[xix]

Greg loves fancy lattes. He buys one every day, leaving $6 each day at the coffee shop. If he'd stop drinking his favorite mocha-smocha, he'd be able to save another $2190 yearly, which would put him into the 15% savings category. He could retire eight years quicker just by downgrading his coffee to a bulky Costco value pack.

It's not hard to notice the impact of cutting one's spending rate. It is much more powerful and easier than increasing one's income. Why? Because cutting spending has double the benefit. On one hand, it increases the amount of money you can save monthly. On the other hand, it permanently decreases the amount you'll need to make each month from your interest.

The math is simple. Do you want to retire in 12 years? Find a way to live only on 40% of your income and invest the rest. Once there, you will not have to work to maintain the lifestyle you have.

The Life-Changing Magic of Compounding

The power of compounding interest and the accompanying rule of 72 is the first big attraction why you should consider investing. In the following paragraphs I will show how anyone can transform small numbers into large ones over time.

What is the rule of 72? To determine how many years an investment will take to double in value, divide 72 by the annual rate of return. For example, an investment that returns 10% doubles every 7.2 years (72/10=7.2). This might not sound overly exciting until you notice that every time the money doubles, it becomes four, then eight, then sixteen, and then thirty-two times more than the initial investment. If you start with one penny and double it every day, by the end of the month it compounds to $5,338,709.12. This is the power of compounding.[xx] Even Albert Einstein deemed it as the greatest mathematical discovery ever.

Let's take a look at an example given by the Bogleheads on compounding. The parents of a newborn baby want to invest in a stock mutual fund that would accumulate into $1,000,000 by the time the baby is 65 years old. With an annual 10% return, can you guess how much these parents need to invest daily to reach this goal? A daily deposit of 54 cents would compound into the desired amount and more in 65 years. "It really helps to start early."

I think that, by now, you understand the power of compounding and the advantage of starting early, and you may wonder, "Yes, I get it, all this sounds amazing! And now what? How do I get started? What should I invest in?" Thank you for asking, I'm about to delve just into this.

I will present you with an investment plan that a 10-year-old would understand and still outperform 90% of finance professionals *in the long run*. It is important to catch the long-run part. Here is an explanation why.

"Until 2008, every 10-year period in the S&P 500's history has had overall positive returns. However, from 2000 to 2009, the market endured a major terrorist attack and a recession. S&P 500 reflected those tough times with an average annual return of -1% and a period of negative returns after that, leading the media to call it the 'lost decade.'

But that's only part of the picture. In the 10-year period right before that (1990–1999) the S&P averaged 18% annually. Put the two decades together, and you get a respectable 8% average annual return. That's why it's so important to have a long-term view about investing instead of looking at the average return each year."[xxi]

To become an informed investor, we need to understand the basic parts of investing.

Inflation

We talked about the life-changing magic of compounding. This magic can turn dark. Inflation works in the opposite direction. You've heard tales from your grandfather of bread for $0.40 a loaf and such, right? Wherever you look today, you can only see bread for $2 (or more). The increase in its price over time is because of inflation. Put plainly, a dollar today simply does not buy as much as it did in your grandpa's time. The last few years, inflation has been about 3% annually.

Let's say you have $1000 and you put it under the bed. A year from now, that $1000 will only be able to buy what $970 did the year before. If you leave it there for another year, it will be $940.09 in today's dollars. Twenty years? That $1000 will only be worth the same as $540.38 today. What about $100,000? Right?

Let's go a step further. In the real world, both the power of compounding and inflation would impact your money. For example, you put your $1000 into a savings account instead of under the pillow. The savings account earns 5.05% APY (very unlikely to have such a high APY, but let's stick to this for now). In twenty years you will have $2670.87. Or will you? Assuming that inflation stays at 3% for the next twenty years, your account balance will actually only have the same buying power as $1450.67 does today. No, we're not done yet.

Let's not forget about taxes. While they only effectively reduce the interest rate that you earn, they will still have an impact on your investment. Say you pay 28% income tax on interest. This means that your effective interest rate on that savings account is 3.63% instead of 5.05 after paying your tax each year. This way, after twenty years, your $1000 will have turned into only $1110.09 in today's dollars. As you can see, any savings account that has a smaller interest than 4% or so is actually losing value over time because of taxes and inflation.[xxii] And trust me, the majority of banks won't pay you 4% interest. Not even 3.

This is why investing—and risking a higher return—is actually not that crazy. The alternative is to lose money, guaranteed, one hundred percent.

Portfolio

"A portfolio is a grouping of financial assets such as stocks, bonds, commodities, currencies, and cash equivalents, as well as their fund counterparts, including mutual, exchange-traded, and closed funds. A portfolio can also consist of non-publicly tradable securities, like real estate, art, and private investments. Money market accounts make full use of this concept to function properly.

Portfolios are held directly by investors and/or managed by financial professionals and money managers. Investors should construct an investment portfolio in accordance with their risk tolerance and investing objectives. Investors can also have multiple portfolios for various purposes. It all depends on one's objectives as an investor."[xxiii]

Diversification

Diversification is a risk management plan that shuffles a great variety of investment products within a portfolio. A well-diversified portfolio has different asset types and investment tools attempting to reduce risk. The rationale behind this technique is that a portfolio constructed of different kinds of assets will, on average, yield higher long-term returns and lower the risk of any individual holding or security.[xxiv]

Stocks

Stocks represent an ownership interest in a corporation. A stock is a small share of a company's business to everyone who purchases it. A stock purchase certificate is issued to the buyer and it marks the number of shares owned. The money invested in stocks is used to fund the activities of the corporation. When all the available stocks for purchase are sold, stocks can be exchanged. One can sell or buy these stocks on the stock exchange the company is present in. This exchange process is usually made by stock brokers who charge a fee (commission) for their involvement.

The value of these shares changes over time—sometimes they are worth more, sometimes less, and they are revalued on a continuous basis when the stock markets are open for trading. What does a stock's value depend on? It depends on how much a new buyer is willing to pay for a share of a company's stock and how much the seller is willing to accept. When a company is strong, trustworthy, and predicted to appreciate, buyers are willing to pay more for a share. If the seller sells their share for a bigger price than what they bought it for, they make a profit. If the seller, however, tries to get rid of their stocks in a time of depreciation and crisis, they might end up getting less money for the share than what they paid for it. In this case, they lose money.

Those investors who hold onto the stocks for long term can benefit from the dividends the company pays occasionally and the increase of the company's value.[xxv]

As a general rule of investment, it is extremely risky to put all your assets in one company's stocks as your returns depend on the performance of that company. If the company goes bankrupt, you can lose all your investments. It's always better to diversify your investments. I will talk about diversification later in this book.

Bonds

When you buy a share of a stock, you become a micro-owner of the company. The company and your money are tied together and they shall rise or fall together. When you buy a bond, you're basically giving a loan for an entity that needs money for something.

When you buy individual bonds at their early issue, you are lending a given sum of your money to the issuer of the bond. In exchange you're promised a certain return on investment, the bond's so-called yield to maturity together with the current value of the bond at a specific time, the so-called maturity date. The length of the maturity date can vary from short term (one year or less), to medium term (two to ten years), to long term (ten years or more).

In other words, a bond is a promise note the issuer gives you in exchange for your money and pays you interest over time until maturity.

Who issues bonds? Multiple entities from the treasury, governmental institutions, companies, mortgage, and municipalities.

For you, as an investor, the biggest risks are credit risk and interest rate risk. Bonds are debts, so if the issuer fails to pay back their debt, the bond can default. Thus, the riskier the issuer, the higher the interest rate will be demanded on the bond (and the greater the cost to the borrower) and vice versa.[xxvi]

The treasury issues are deemed to be the safest bonds as the government supports them. They include notes, bonds, bills, TIPS (treasury inflation-protected securities), and two kinds of US savings bonds (EE bonds and I bonds). Treasury interest income is exempt from local and state taxes.

Understanding Stocks and Bonds

Even though I read a lot of definitions about stocks and bonds, I was always a little bit unsure if I understood well what they were and the risk I'd be exposed to if I purchase either. A word of caution, my definitions above are far from exhaustive—my purpose is only to help you understand what they are. If you wish to go deep into the specifics of stocks and bonds, read the book *The Bogleheads' Guide to Investing*.

The best portrayal of their difference came from a book I recently read, called *If You Can* by William J Bernstein. He defines stocks and bonds as follows:

"Say you're starting a business. It'll be a bit before it starts making money, but from day one it'll have expenses, and you'll need money for that up front.

You can get that money in one of two ways: you can borrow it from relatives, friends, or from a bank, or you can sell an ownership interest to a friend or family member. For example, if your brother is half owner, he's entitled to half of all of your business' future earnings.

Nothing prevents you from doing both, in fact that is what most large corporations do. If you do both borrow money *and* sell shares, then both legally and morally, you have to pay the lenders' interest and principal first. Only after they have been paid, and only after your other ongoing business expenses have been met, can you then pay out the remaining profits to you and your brother.

You and your brother are thus the "residual owners" of the business; if, and only if, you can pay off your lenders and your expenses do you make any money. *From the investor's perspective, an ownership stake (a stock) is much riskier than a loan to your business (a bond), and so a stock deserves a higher expected return than a bond.*"[xxvii]

Index

When stock brokers talk about "beating the market," they usually mean to outperform certain stock indexes. An index basically is a certain amount of stocks thrown in a bucket. The S&P 500 is an index, for example, which includes the top-performing companies in the U.S. Companies like Exxon, Apple, and Microsoft are parts of this index. Experts measure daily how each of the 500 stocks performed, and based on this data, they expose to the public if the price of 500 stocks collectively went up or down.

Indexes diminish the risk of buying into individual

stocks. You buy all 500 of them all at once when you buy a share of the S&P500. Some of these 500 companies will perform better, some worse, but overall your money will be safer. If all 500 companies in the S&P 500 go bankrupt at the same time... let's just say you'll have greater problems than losing all your investments.

What you're buying into is the historical data of the resiliency of these top-performing companies. Wars, depressions, pandemics came and went and the S&P 500 always recovered. And if a company failed to keep up with the standard, it got replaced with another, better-performing company.

Why Are Actively Managed Funds Unnecessary for the Average Investor (Or above Average, Even)?

Investing in an index is great for rookies because Standard & Poor's experts already selected the top-performing companies. It is needless to pay a financial professional to pick them for you. This being said, there are a variety of indexes out there, not just the S&P 500.

Take the Vanguard 500 created by Jack Bogle, for example, which mirrors the S&P 500. Just to prove to you that in the long run investing in an index fund such as these pays off better for the average investor, I share with you the following story.

Robert Arnott, the founder of Research Affiliates, engaged in a 20-year study where he closely monitored the top 200 actively managed funds (funds that are 24/7 adjusted and modified by experts trying to beat the market) that managed at least $100 million. The results were mind-blowing. Out of the 200 fund managers, only eight managed to beat the Vanguard 500 Index. Eight. Those odds are worse than 4%. Even a clock that has stopped shows the accurate time twice a day.[xxviii]

A mutual fund is a type of investment. It pools together the money of many people. At the top of it is a fund manager (a person or a company) whose task is to invest the money. It varies by each fund, but generally the manager invests in a mixture of stocks, bonds, and money market instruments. We call them securities.

Mutual funds are advantageous because the risk is reduced through diversification. I mentioned before that buying individual stocks is not a great idea for the laymen, or anyone, really, who can't afford to lose a lot of money. Diversification is the antidote for a large part of investment risk.

When you buy into a mutual fund, you're purchasing a share of it and you become a shareholder with all the other people who invest in it. The net asset value (NAV) is the price at which you can purchase or sell a share.

How to Choose a Mutual Fund

While widely diversified mutual funds are less risky than individual investment ventures, it's almost impossible to pick a guaranteed winner. A stock that has done well last year may not do so well this year. Air carriers and tourism-related stocks performed quite well before but are rolling at rock bottom now, just to give you an actual example. In other words, there is no investment strategy that will constantly be a winner. If someone tells you otherwise, don't believe them; including the prestigious economist, last year's baller investor, or your uncle. Another golden rule of investment is that you won't get a high reward without high risk. So if anyone promises you a wild return with minimal or no risk to "beat the market," be suspicious.

Money market funds are one kind of mutual fund. They are a safer alternative to a bank's savings account as they pay a higher interest than most banks on savings and are the safest, most stable type of mutual fund. They are different than the MMAs (money market accounts) we learned about in the chapter on savings. The most important difference is that the money you put in an MMF is *not* federally insured like a regular savings account. That being said, only two MMFs have lost money ever since their creation in 1970. One of these was a fund called Reserve Primary Fund, which lost money in 2008 because it held money market instruments from Lehman Brothers, the bank giant which declared bankruptcy.[xxix] MMFs also have a minimum starting balance of $1,000 usually.

Money market funds invest in money market instruments, as a general rule, with greater success than Reserve Primary Fund. Money market instruments are usually issued by trusted corporations or governments when they need money for the short term.

There are many types of MMFs. Taxable money market funds make the most sense to buy when you're in a low tax bracket as you need to pay federal taxes on the dividends you earn. Taxable MMFs include U.S. Treasury money funds (Treasury bills), U.S. government money funds, and corporate money funds. There are also tax-exempt money market funds, namely federal tax-exempt money funds, double tax-exempt money funds (exempt of both federal and state income tax), and triple tax-exempt money funds (exempt of federal, state, and city taxes).

Whenever you invest in a money market fund, there are two main things to consider: your risk tolerance and taxes. If you want to play it safe, choose a U.S. Treasury MMF. For a higher yield, you need to take some risk and choose a corporate MMF. However, the yield in your hand can differ from the yield you get on paper. The difference is made by the tax you owe.

Let me give you a simple example. Let's say you want to invest in a corporate MMF that yields 6%. I will assume that you owe only federal tax and you're in the 20% tax bracket. So, you'll need to pay 20% of that 6%, or 1.2% of what you earn, to Uncle Sam. Therefore the actual value of the 6% yield is 4.8% (6% minus 1.2%). If a tax-exempt MMF pays 5%, it might be a better option for you. Keep in mind that yields on MMFs change over time, so make this calculation at least yearly. If you discover that you'd earn more in a taxable account than in the tax-exempt account, transfer your money there.[xxx]

To learn more about mutual funds, read Jack Bogle's *Common Sense and Mutual Funds*. It is a dense, 600-page monster of a book, but it is organized in chapters that work as individual essays. Use the book as a reference guide and read only what you need at the moment rather than aiming for a cover-to-cover marathon.

ETFs

An exchange-traded fund (ETF) is a collection of securities that are quite similar to mutual funds but trade on an exchange, just like a stock. ETF share prices oscillate all day as they are bought and sold. Mutual funds only trade once a day after the market closes. ETFs usually track an underlying index, but they can also invest in other industry sectors. A more popular ETF is SDPR S&P 500, which tracks the S&P 500 Index.

An ETF is a fund that includes a variety of underlying assets instead of only one like a stock. Because there are more types of assets within an ETF, they can be a good selection for diversification. They can contain all types of investments including stocks, commodities, or bonds. Some ETFs have U.S.-only holdings, while others are international.[xxxi]

ETFs became increasingly popular in the past years partially for their diversification potential and partially for their general low cost.

Retirement Plans

This section will be more interesting for my readers from the U.S. Retirement plans in the U.S. will offer you a tax advantage—either at the beginning or when you're withdrawing. If you invest in a 401(k), you are putting your pre-tax money in them, reducing your taxable income. However, when you withdraw money from here, you'll need to pay taxes. If you choose a Roth IRA (individual retirement account), you do the saving phase with after-tax money—but the withdrawal is tax free.

There are other benefits to retirement savings plans, like contribution matching from one's employer to 401(k) plans.

People often wonder which plan they should choose. Here is the short answer: If your company matches contributions, go for a 401(k) and try to maximize it. It's basically free money. Make sure to take full advantage of your company's match. To secure your retirement better with a 401(k), increase your annual contribution, as roughly half of 401(k) plans with automatic enrollment options use a standard savings rate of only 3%. Experts advise to try to push the yearly savings rate to 15%.[xxxii] If you can afford it, also fund an IRA.

If you're self-employed, you also have several retirement savings options to choose from. In addition to the plans described below for rank-and-file workers as well as entrepreneurs, you can also invest in a Roth IRA or traditional IRA, subject to certain income limits, which have smaller annual contribution limits than most other plans.

1. Defined Contribution Plans

The 401(k) plan is the most common defined contribution plan. All types of employers use it. The 403(b) plan has a similar structure, but it is offered to employees of public schools and certain tax-exempt organizations. The 457(b) plan is usually given to state and local governments. The contribution limit for each of them is $19,500 in 2020 ($26,000 for those age 50 and over).[xxxiii]

Some defined contribution plans have a Roth option, meaning you can use after-tax dollars to contribute, but you can withdraw the money tax-free when you retire. It makes the most sense to choose this plan if you estimate that you'll be in a higher tax bracket when you retire than where you are now.

Let's see the specifics of each plan:

188

401(k) Plans

A 401(k) plan is a tax-advantaged plan. Contributions are not considered taxable income. The employee collects their savings from pre-tax money and the plan allows their contributions to grow tax-free until they're withdrawn at retirement. Early withdrawals (before age 59 ½) may be penalized with additional taxes.

Choose a 401(k) plan if you wish to save for retirement in an easy way. You can schedule automatic investments where a part of your paycheck directly goes to your 401(k) account. You can invest the money accumulated here in high-return assets such as stocks and you don't have to pay taxes on them until you retire. Plus, your employer may offer you a match on your contributions, which helps you grow your savings at double speed.

The drawback of 401(k) plans is that early withdrawal is penalized. You can't touch the money even in an emergency—only at a high cost. Also, your investment opportunities are limited to your employer's 401(k) program, so you may not be able to buy the assets you want.

Overall, a 401(k) is still one of the best retirement plans.

403(b) Plans

A 403(b) plan has the same attributives as a 401(k) plan, but it's offered by public schools, charities, and some churches, just to name a few. A 403(b) plan is one of the best ways for you to save for retirement if you work in the aforementioned sectors.

457(b) Plans

A 457(b) plan is similar to a 401(k), but it's available only for employees of state and local governments and some tax-exempt organizations. In addition, this plan provides some special savings provisions for older workers, and early withdrawals (before the age of 59 ½) are not subject to penalties. On the downside, they usually don't offer an employer match.

2. IRA Plans

The individual retirement account (IRA) was created by the U.S. government to help people save for retirement. Individuals can contribute up to $6,000 to an account in 2020, and those over age 50 can contribute up to $7,000. There are multiple types of IRAs. Here I will talk about the traditional IRA, Roth IRA, spousal IRA, rollover IRA, SEP IRA, and SIMPLE IRA.

Traditional IRA

A traditional IRA is a tax-advantaged plan, which gives substantial tax breaks while you save for retirement. Anyone who makes money by working can contribute to the plan with a pre-tax payment. This means that initial contributions are not taxable income. The IRA allows these contributions to grow tax-free until you withdraw them at retirement. Then they become taxable. Earlier withdrawals may lead to additional taxes and penalties.

The upside of a traditional IRA is that it offers great tax benefits, and it also hardly limits the purchase of a number of investments—stocks, bonds, CDs, real estate among others. On the downside, early withdrawals can be quite costly. Also, you will need to invest your money yourself. Still, if your employer doesn't offer a defined contribution plan, a traditional IRA is a good choice of retirement plan.

Roth IRA

Contributions to a Roth IRA, in contrast to a traditional one, are made with after-tax money. In other words, you pay taxes first, invest after. In exchange, you won't have to pay tax on any contributions and earnings that come out of the account when you retire. An upside to a Roth IRA is that you can touch your contributions (not earnings) before retirement without being penalized. On the downside, just as with traditional IRAs, you will have to do the investing for yourself (or hire someone to do it for you).

Spousal IRA

Spousal IRA allows the spouse of a worker with earned income to fund an IRA. The working spouse's taxable income must be more than the contributions made to any IRAs. It can be both a traditional IRA or a Roth IRA. The greatest advantage of such an IRA is that a nonworking spouse can also enjoy the IRA's many benefits.

Rollover IRA

You create a rollover IRA when you relocate a retirement account (401(k) or IRA) to a new IRA account. Basically, you "roll" the money from one account to the other. You get to keep the advantage of the tax benefits of an IRA. You can create a rollover IRA at any institution that allows you. The rollover IRA can be both a traditional IRA or a Roth IRA—plus, you can switch the account types with the rollover from traditional to Roth or vice versa. There's no limit to the amount of money that can be transferred into a rollover IRA. Some transfers can create tax liabilities. Make sure to understand the consequences before you transfer any money. The best part of a rollover IRA is that it allows you to keep the benefits of a 401(k) plan, for example, if you decide to leave your workplace.

194

SEP IRA

The SEP IRA is set up like a traditional IRA, but for small business owners and their employees. Self-employed individuals can also set up a SEP IRA, and its higher contribution limits make them much more attractive than a regular IRA. Contribution limits in 2020 are 25 percent of compensation or $57,000, whichever is less.

Resist the urge to touch the money ahead of time as you'll likely have to pay a 10% penalty on top of income tax.[xxxiv]

SIMPLE IRA

With 401(k) plans, employers have to go through a number of nondiscrimination tests each year. This is necessary to make sure that highly compensated workers aren't contributing too much to the plan relative to the rank and file. The SIMPLE IRA provides the same benefits to all employees so this roadblock is avoided. The employer can choose to contribute a 3% match or make a 2% nonelective contribution even if the employee saves nothing. Most SIMPLE IRAs are designed to provide a match. However, the employee contribution is limited to $13,500 for 2020 (other defined contribution plans allow $19,500).

What Should You Do with All the Information You Learned Above?

That's up to you. Investing is not without risk. I'm sure I've delivered that message thus far. But not investing and allowing inflation to slowly devour the buying power of our money is also not great. In the following paragraphs I will share with you the best advice experts give to laypeople like you and me on how to invest for our retirement.

Here is what William J. Bernstein has to say:

"Start by saving 15% of your salary at the age of 25 into a 401(k) plan, an IRA, or a taxable account (or all three). Put equal amounts of that 15% into just three different mutual funds:

- A U.S. stock market index fund
- An international total stock market index fund
- A U.S. total bond market index fund

Overtime, the three funds will grow at different rates, so once per year you'll adjust their amounts so that they're again equal. (That's fifteen minutes per year assuming you've enrolled in an automatic savings   plan.)

That's it."

Bernstein continues by assuring us that if we follow this simple rule during our working career, we'll outperform most professional investors and we'll retire comfortably. The problem is, not many people are able to follow this simple formula.

Why? A few things...

Quite counterintuitively, when we have a bull market and we buy in the stock market, the expected returns are not so high. In a bear market (when the economy sucks), should we buy like crazy, that's when we can cash in large growth as the market slowly recovers. People work in reverse. When prices start to drop, what does the average Joe do? He sells like his life depends on it; he believes it actually does. He often sells his shares with a net loss. "I'd better save what I still can." Then the market eventually recovers. Our Joe starts to feel more secure about it again. So he buys shares again, at a higher price.

I know it is the hardest to resist selling when the market goes down. I know that when you invested

$50,000, and in five years it went up to $60,000, and then suddenly is down to $40,000, you panic. Where will it stop? $30,000? $20,000? It makes more sense to save the $40,000 while you can. Even if you face a loss. But learn from history. The market always recovered. Always. Even after the Great Depression. Even after 2008. It might take some time. Two years, five years… but it will bounce back, and you won't lose a penny.

That's why it is so important to invest only the money that you won't need in the next 10 to 20 years.

That's why it is so important to invest in accordance with your risk tolerance.

That's why it is so important to read about and learn   from   history.

Don't follow the sheep. Is your uncle freaking out about investing at the stock market now? Great!

That's a good sign. Whatever the majority preaches, in investment it's better to do the opposite.

How should you allocate the funds in your portfolio? First of all, set a financial goal. What are you investing for? Retirement? Quick cash? How much you need? How quickly do you want to get there? How much can you invest to reach this goal? How much risk are you willing to take?

A rule of thumb of allocation is subtracting your age out of 100. Invest your age in bonds and the rest in stocks. For example, I'm 29. 100-29=71. I should invest 71% of my funds in stocks and the rest in bonds. It's said that as you age, it's better to have more and more money in bonds as they are safer—but yield less. Investing aggressively in your youth is better because you have time to recover if stuff hits the fan.

For example, the stock market fell deeply low in

March 2020. To me, whatever losses I experienced are okay because I don't need the money and the market will certainly recover before my age of retirement. To my 60-year-old uncle, this fall was a tragedy because he wanted to retire in two years. The market might not recover fully within two years. Unfortunately, he didn't follow the golden rule of asset allocation and had more stocks than his age would have warranted it. So, he lost a lot, and now he's anxious—and for the right reasons. Had he kept 60% of his portfolio in bonds, he would have fared better.

Investing is a gamble. But there are many little things you can do to minimize your risks. Burt Malkiel, an investor well in his eighties, lived through all phases and walks of market changes. In his widely acknowledged classic book on investment, *A Random Walk Down Wall Street*, he centers the reader's attention around the following point: trying to time and beat the market is a loser's game. Indexing, or passive investing if you may, doesn't try to beat the market. It mimics or matches the market.

At the end of the day there are only two types of assets you can invest in: high risk–high reward ones (stocks) and low risk–low reward ones (CDs, MMFs, T-Bills). Your job is to accurately and honestly assess your risk tolerance and diversify your portfolio accordingly. You can diversify your portfolio by choosing to invest in index funds (preferably no-load, low-cost, tax-efficient, low-trading-cost ones).

Even so, don't underestimate the stress and anxiety of losing a big chunk of real money you once used to own. This being said, don't underestimate the power of inflation either.

Chapter 7: The 1-Page Budget

It must feel weird that we've talked about so many aspects of money management so far but we haven't touch the budgeting part. Yet. That's because I wanted to illustrate to you what you can win and lose if you choose to adopt or skip keeping a budget. Now you are well equipped with information, so I really hope that you're actually excited to learn how to set up an effective budget. Now, you probably know what the things you want to budget for are, and what things you'd like to spend less on. Let's dig into our final but arguably most important chapter...

According to the *Business Dictionary*, budgeting is "an estimate of costs, revenues, and resources over a specified period, reflecting a reading of future financial conditions and goals." In other words, budgeting is the method of making a plan on how to spend your money.

We live in a world where money matters and money talks. Shortage of money screams. More heartbreaks and attacks happen because of the stress coming from a lack of financial security than any other source of stress. We don't want any heart-related problem here, we want peace of mind. To get there, we need to use our brains.

When you create your spending plan and start using it, your life becomes transparent. You'll be able to track what you've spent your money on item by item, day by day. If you still want to cut expenses, you will have a clear picture of where you can make these changes. In the first couple months you'll track your spending retrospectively. Hopefully, as the months progress, you'll switch this routine into knowing in advance what you'll spend your money on. When you get familiar with living on your budget, you can try mapping out your finances for three to six months in advance. This is budget planning.

Estimate all the income and expenses you'll have in the next few months. This way you can easily forecast in which months you will need to tighten your budget, and which months are those where you'll have extra money.

In most cases, expenses month by month aren't linear. You'll need to think ahead, forecast, and plan your budget to even out the highs and lows in your finances almost every time. It is just a matter of practice to do it well, and quite quickly you'll be able to manage your life stress free. Making a budget plan three to six to twelve months in advance helps you forecast how much money you can realistically save. It is critical to be honest and realistic when you make your plans. If you have a low income but lots of essential expenses, it is not realistic to hope for saving more than 50% monthly. You can, however, see clearly that your income in the present won't allow you the lifestyle you want to live, even with tightening your belt and saving like crazy. A budget, therefore, can also reveal to you the ugly truth about your finances, and can motivate you to study, learn new skills, and change to a job with a higher income. Or look for alternative moneymakers like passive income sources.

Creating a budget is important to get yourself out of debt, to keep yourself from getting into debt again, to accumulate savings, to invest money… Oh, if only we could save for all those things. We want a lot of things, yet many of us struggle with creating a budget and sticking to it. Like in many other areas of life, there is no one-size-fits-all budgeting plan. But you can experiment.

I am a long-time budgeter. I tried so many methods. The one that works the best for me, and thus I recommend to you wholeheartedly, is the zero budgeting method.

What does "zero budgeting method" mean? It means that you are giving every dollar a job. To explain it further, it means that you budget every dollar of your income to exactly match your expenses.

Now, wait up a second, this doesn't mean that you get to spend every dollar you make on lousy things! This budgeting takes your income and divides it among your expenses, including the money you are putting into your savings account. This method is perfect for those who want to completely control their money. Control freaks, put your hands up. Mine are high above my head. Using this method, you can micromanage your money in a good way so that you know exactly where your money is going.

If you work the same number of hours every month (or more or less the same if you have a job with heavy overtime duty) or if you are paid a salary, you have a fixed income. When your income doesn't vary every paycheck, you should have a pretty good idea about how much money you can play with, and a good handle on where each dollar goes. But it might be time to change how you are budgeting if you don't have good savings.

There is a default budgeting method promoted by Mint, the 50/30/20 budget. Basically, 50% of your income stands for your essential expenses, 30% could be used for personal expenses, and 20% should be put directly into your savings. These three things add up to 100% of your income without a dollar to spare. This is a great place to start your budgeting journey.

But I would add a tweak to this idea. Keep the categories, essential expenses, personal expenses, and savings—but ditch the percentages. Use your priorities as a guideline instead. If you want to live your best life today (and by best I mean with the most indulgences) keep the 50/30/20 ratio. But if you want to build up for the future more, become aggressive with your savings (debt repayment and investing). I would say do a 50/10/40 or even 40/10/50 ratio in your early years. This would mean that you keep your essential spending low— you don't buy a new car, you maybe live in rentals or with roommates as long as it's a feasible option, and you pour most of your income into your savings. We saw how powerful it can be if you start investing early in life. The less debt you hoard together early in life, the less you need to pay off—so the more you can invest. Of course, this only applies if financial security and eventually financial freedom is your main financial priority.

At first glance, you may think that 50% is a little high for essential expenses, but most people actually struggle with keeping their essentials to 50% of their income. Essentials include everything from your housing bills, student loans, other debts, and even the butter on your morning toast! If you can stick to 50% for your essentials, you are doing a great job.

Because this budget is dividing the income you already have, it is easily adaptable for many people. It also takes the guesswork out of budgeting. Instead of saving X amount of dollars a month, you are saving a percentage of your income. As your income grows, so does your savings! This is helpful because you don't have to keep track of the dollar amount you are putting into your savings each month.

Now it's time to divide your own income. You didn't think I was going to let you get off that easy, did you? Grab the sheet of paper that hopefully by now has your monthly income, your recurring essential expenses, and a rough estimate of your other expenses.

Let's say you make $1,000 a paycheck and you get paid every two weeks. So, if we follow the percentage of Mint, for the first two weeks you have $500 for essentials, $300 for personal expenses, and you're going to be putting $200 into your savings account. While I'm a fan of different percentages as I'm a fan of the idea of financial independence, if you can start dividing your income into these three categories with these percentages, you're already doing well.

Take a look at your piece of paper you had with all of your monthly expenses written down. Look at these numbers and look at what you get paid each paycheck. Do the numbers match up? Will you be able to fit your expenses into these percentages?

If your essentials are taking up 60% of your income and you are spending the other 40% on personal expenses, it's time to cut out a few things. Maybe that means you go a few weeks longer before going to the hair salon, or cutting out your twice-weekly bar night. The personal expense category is where you can cut out a lot of unnecessary items.

The goal here is to get as much as you can into your savings. By saving more, you set yourself up for less stress down the road.

I'm living the entrepreneurial life, so I never know what I'm going to be making the next month. This can be really stressful if I don't have a good grip on my spending habits. Not every month will be my best month. I have to be prepared—mentally and financially—to survive the shoestring months. I'm lucky in one aspect, though: I get paid with a sixty-day delay. This means that I know sixty days in advance what I am going to make two months later. This allows me to forecast and adjust my budget far ahead of time without any hiccups.

Individuals with variable incomes have a hard time spending. As the game goes, when you make more money, you might be tempted to spend more. Not the best idea. This is where using percentages for budgeting can prove problematic. 50% of $1000 is $500. If, for some reason, the next month you make $2000, it would mean that you could spend $1000 on essentials. If you are a strict rule follower but you don't mind taking advantage of the fine print disclosures, you might jump on the occasion to indulge in the extra cash and spend it recklessly. You're right, it's within your budget. But if you lived just fine on $500 last month, it's not necessary to spend the extra cash. It could, however, go a much longer way if it's reinvested in paying off your debts, growing your emergency fund, or buying a few more assets to invest in.

Adopt a saving mindset around your budget. Most of us mistakenly think that the saving mindset is what poor people have. They are all about saving money, stressing their soul out because of the lack of money. How do you start each day? "What do I need to spend on today?" or, "What can I buy today?" or, "What can I afford today?" These questions reflect different levels of a scarcity-spending mindset.

People who wake up thinking how much they can save or what their actual needs are vs. wants are those who sooner or later won't have financial headaches. Not everybody becomes a billionaire, but that's not the goal of personal financing. The goal of personal financing is keeping more money in your pocket than your monthly expenses, make some of your money work for you, and you eventually stop working as a necessity. Personal finances help you develop a healthy financial mindset and help you to never have money issues again.

So even when you have a good month and you cash in more than you expected, you need to keep the saving mindset. Don't worry, the saving mindset makes rich people rich, and poor people rich too. The simplest method to save money and gain financial freedom is to not spend mindlessly, save/invest the most you can with the best interest–risk balance. Some of my months are really great and others are pretty bad. So how do I manage to save?

I use the Mint method with the percentages as an indicator for how I should compartmentalize my income. But, I don't stick to the percentages. I stick to numbers.

The budgeting method I use consists of three groups, net disposable income, total expenditure, and savings. Net disposable income is a fancy way of saying "income." The total expenditure group has different sub-categories, including business expenses. Each of these categories have a strict cap, and I take it very seriously. I don't spend beyond my cap. I chose my categories because they cover my lifestyle's expenses the best. You might not need the same categories I do. Choose categories that best suit your needs.

My savings group has two sub-groups. I'm blessed enough that I'm debt free (I only had a student loan of about $1,500 or so and never again). I also have a six-month cushion of emergency funds. And I have another savings account where I keep liquid cash because I'm paranoid and I wouldn't want to invest all my money minus the emergency fund. Even if I'm painfully aware of the power of inflation, I can't make myself get rid of my "emergency emergency" fund. That's just my way of dealing with the high risk I play with on the stock market having 85% of my investments in well-diversified stock index funds. I know I'm talking against myself right now. Remember, according to experts, I should use the 100-my age=stocks–bonds ratio, but hey, I didn't start saving at the age of 25. I need to make up for those lost four years. Follow my risky example at your own risk. Needless to say, I'm not the happiest right now as the current pandemic devours the stock market. But I don't sell. Quite the contrary, I'm buying stocks in a balanced, calculated way week by week, doing something called dollar-cost averaging. This means that some weeks I will pay more for my stocks, some weeks I will pay less, but as I can't guess the market, over time I pay a stable price for them. So my two sub-groups for savings are my personal retirement fund contribution and my investments.

Why do I work with numbers instead of percentages? Because in my view, a percentage, say, 30% of your income for personal expenses, can trap you into overspending or spending money on useless crap that won't make you happy even in the short run. You may be one of the more conscientious ones and put into your savings whatever you have left in each of your categories. But you could be a money-munching monster like me who maxes out all of her categories, neatly rationalizing the reasons behind it. I know I'm like that. But I also know I'm notoriously rule abiding. So I will respect the red lines of my cap limits. If I left my personal expense category unspecified with a 30% income limit, most certainly I'd spend all that money on clothes and makeup. Ouch. But as I name this category "Clothes and Makeup" and I put a $100 cap on it, I will not spend more on these things.

My way of budgeting is actually a no-waste, shopaholic-proof way to freedom. I'm not intuitive with good money management practices. I never saw a good role model I could mimic. I think many of us are in the same boat. So I had to find a way to control my inner spendthrift.

Without further ado, here is your one-page budget plan:

The 1-Page Budgeting Plan

Net Disposable Income: _____ (total)

- ❖ Source 1:
- ❖ Source 2:
- ❖ Source 3:

Total Expenditure: _____ (cap)

- ❖ Business: _____ (cap)
  - o Ads: _____
  - o Promotions: _____
  - o Book Editing: _____

- ❖ Rent: _____ (cap)

- ❖ Beauty & Shopping: _____ (cap)
  - o Clothes: _____
  - o Makeup: _____

- o Beauty Services: _____

- ❖ Daily Living: _____ (cap)
    - o Food: _____
        - ▪ Grocery Shopping: _____
        - ▪ Kombucha: _____
        - ▪ Coffee: _____
    - o Household items: _____
    - o Utilities: _____

- ❖ Transportation: _____ (cap)
    - o Gas: _____
    - o Uber: _____

- ❖ Entertainment: _____ (cap)

- ❖ Health Care: _____(cap)
    - o Therapist: _____
    - o Books: _____
    - o Courses: _____

Total Savings: _____ (NO CAP)

❖ Retirement Plan: 40% of my total savings

❖ Investments: 60% of my total savings

That's it. So simple, yet very effective. You can turn your one-page budget into a 20-page budget if you keep track of every item you purchase, neatly putting them into their rightful category. Take a look at the group *Daily Living* → *Food* → *Grocery Shopping*. It's broken down nicely so I can track what exactly I spend money on. If you think I'm doing this on paper, you're wrong. I use an app which models quite well my budgeting intentions. It's called iSaveMoney. Find the link to it at the end of this chapter.

As an entrepreneur, I can't be very sure how much I will make month to month, so I can't cap everything. This is why I left my savings open. I live well, in my opinion (and that's what matters), but some might consider my lifestyle weirdly Spartan.

You may tell me, "But aren't you supposed to pay yourself first, meaning, separate your savings?" You're right. If I had a fixed income, that's what I'd do, and that's what I advise you to do if you have one. With variable income, however, your safest bet might be to keep your expenses as low as possible with a strict cap and throw all the "leftovers" into savings. This is how it works best for me. I avoid owning a car (I pay my share of my boyfriend's gas bill), so I bike or walk to most places. I used to use UberPool when I absolutely had to. I'm happy with renting a smaller flat, I make my own coffee, we cook our fancy meals at home, I sew the holes on my socks... you know, you don't need that much.

Yes, if I had a huge income cut from one month to another, I would need to lower the caps on my categories—even get rid of some to still be able to save some money. But to get to such a drastic pay cut, Amazon would need to collapse or something, which is highly unlikely.

But again, this budgeting method is my bulletproof recipe. Try it. If you like it, use it. Tailor it to your needs. If you have kids, aging parents, or a chronic illness, your budget will look wildly differently than mine. The guiding principles, however, should be the same. Spend less than what you make. Save for emergencies, retirement, and other objectives.

There are some very good apps and online resources that you can use if you don't like my one-page budget:

-	Mint's free budget templates: https://www.mint.com/budgeting-3/keep-track-of-your-finances-with-a-free-budget-template

- iSaveMoney (An app available for Android. I use this one.): https://isavemoney.app

- EveryDollar (An app available for Android and iOS. Another great zero-based budgeting app.): https://www.everydollar.com/

At the end of the day, it doesn't matter how you budget as long as you do it following this basic principle: Spend less than what you earn. Flip back for a moment to your one-, five-, ten-, twenty-years-in-the-future goals. Based on what you learned about better yielding savings accounts, investments, and budgeting, how much do you need to save in order to achieve what you want?

Final Words

The path of financial freedom doesn't need to be complicated. Spend less. Track your expenses diligently, diversify them, and put a cap on them. And most importantly, don't overspend your caps. Pay off your debts. Have an emergency fund. Invest the money you won't need in the next 10-20 years in diversified portfolios. Keep the rest of your savings in high APY (annual percentage yield) savings accounts or CDs. Give every dollar a job. Let them work for you.

Let this book work for you.

Love,

Zoe

Before you go...

How did you like this book? Would you consider leaving a feedback about your reading experience so other readers could know about it? If you would sacrifice some of your time to do so, there are several options you can do it:

1. Please leave a review on Amazon.
2. Please leave a review on goodreads.com. Here is a link to my profile where you find all of my books. https://www.goodreads.com/author/show/14967542.Zoe_McKey
3. Send me a private message to zoemckey@gmail.com
4. Tell your friends and family about your reading experience.

Your feedback is very valuable to me to assess if I'm on the good path providing help to you and where do I need to improve. Your feedback is also valuable to other people as they can learn about my work and perhaps give an independent author as myself a chance. I deeply appreciate any kind of feedback you take time to provide me.

Thank you so much for choosing to read my book among the many out there. If you'd like to receive an update once I have a new book, you can subscribe to my newsletter at www.zoemckey.com. You'll get my *Self-Discovery Starter Kit* for FREE. You'll also get occasional book recommendations from other authors I trust and know they deliver good quality books.

Brave Enough

Time to learn how to overcome the feeling of inferiority and achieve success. Brave Enough takes you step by step through the process of understanding the nature of your fears, overcome limiting beliefs and gain confidence with the help of studies, personal stories and actionable exercises at the end of each chapter.

Say goodbye to fear of rejection and inferiority complex once and for all.

Less Mess Less Stress

Don't compromise with your happiness. "Good enough" is not the life you deserve - you deserve the best, and the good news is that you can have it. Learn the surprising truth that it's not by doing more, but less with Less Mess Less Stress.

We know that we own too much, we say yes for too many engagements, and we stick to more than we should. Physical, mental and relationship clutter are daily burdens we have to deal with. Change your mindset and live a happier life with less.

Minimalist Budget

Minimalist Budget will help you to turn your bloated expenses into a well-toned budget, spending on exactly what you need and nothing else.

This book presents solutions for two major problems in our consumer society: (1) how to downsize your cravings without having to sacrifice the fun stuff, and (2) how to whip your finances into shape and follow a personalized budget.

Rewire Your Habits

230

Rewire Your Habits discusses which habits one should adopt to make changes in 5 life areas: self-improvement, relationships, money management, health, and free time. The book addresses every goal-setting, habit building challenge in these areas and breaks them down with simplicity and ease.

Tame Your Emotions

Tame Your Emotions is a collection of the most common and painful emotional insecurities and their antidotes. Even the most successful people have fears and self-sabotaging habits. But they also know how to use them to their advantage and keep their fears on a short leash. This is exactly what my book will teach you – using the tactics of experts and research-proven methods.

Emotions can't be eradicated. But they can be controlled.

The Art of Minimalism

The Art of Minimalism will present you 4 minimalist techniques, the bests from around the world, to give you a perspective on how to declutter your house, your mind, and your life in general. Learn how to let go of everything that is not important in your life and find methods that give you a peace of mind and happiness instead.

Keep balance at the edge of minimalism and consumerism.

The Critical Mind

If you want to become a critical, effective, and rational thinker instead of an irrational and snap-judging one, this book is for you. Critical thinking skills strengthen your decision making muscle, speed up your analysis and judgment, and help you spot errors easily.

The Critical Mind offers a thorough introduction to the rules and principles of critical thinking. You will find widely usable and situation-specific advice on how to critically approach your daily life, business, friendships, opinions, and even social media.

The Disciplined Mind

Where you end up in life is determined by a number of times you fall and get up, and how much pain and discomfort you can withstand along the way. The path to an extraordinary accomplishment and a life worth living is not innate talent, but focus, willpower, and disciplined action.

Maximize your brain power and keep in control of your thoughts.

In The Disciplined Mind, you will find unique lessons through which you will learn those essential steps and qualities that are needed to reach your goals easier and faster.

The Mind-Changing Habit of Journaling

Understand where your negative self-image, bad habits, and unhealthy thoughts come from. Know yourself to change yourself. Embrace the life-changing transformation potential of journaling. This book shows you how to use the ultimate self-healing tool of journaling to find your own answers to your most pressing problems, discover your true self and lead a life of growth mindset.

The Unlimited Mind

This book collects all the tips, tricks and tactics of the most successful people to develop your inner smartness.

The Unlimited Mind will show you how to think smarter and find your inner genius. This book is a collection of research and scientific studies about better decision-making, fairer judgments, and intuition improvement. It takes a critical look at our everyday cognitive habits and points out small but serious mistakes that are easily correctable.

Who You Were Meant To Be

Discover the strengths of your personality and how to use them to make better life choices. In Who You Were Born To Be, you'll learn some of the most influential personality-related studies.

Thanks to these studies you'll learn to capitalize on your strengths, and how you can you become the best version of yourself.

Wired For Confidence

Do you feel like you just aren't good enough? End this vicious thought cycle NOW. Wired For Confidence tells you the necessary steps to break out from the pits of low self-esteem, lowered expectations, and lack of assertiveness. Take the first step to creating the life you only dared to dream of.

References

Bernstein, William J. If You Can. William J Bernstein. 2014.

Danko, D William. Stanley, J Thomas. The Millionaire Next Door. Taylor Trade Publishing. 2010.

Hamm, Trent. Compound Interest Versus Inflation: The Battle For Your Money. The Simple Dollar. 2019. https://www.thesimpledollar.com/investing/blog/compound-interest-versus-inflation-the-battle-for-your-money/

Investopedia. Diversification. Investopedia. 2020. https://www.investopedia.com/terms/d/diversification.asp

Investopedia. ETF. Investopedia. 2020.
https://www.investopedia.com/terms/e/etf.asp

Investopedia. Portfolio. Investopedia. 2020.
https://www.investopedia.com/terms/p/portfolio.as
p

Investopedia. The Basics of Bonds. Investopedia.
2020. https://www.investopedia.com/financial-
edge/0312/the-basics-of-bonds.aspx

Johnson, Angela. "76% of Americans are living
paycheck-to-paycheck." CNN. 2013.
http://money.cnn.com/2013/06/24/pf/emergency-
savings/index.html

Kobliener, Beth. Get a Financial Life. Simon &
Schuster. 2009.

Lindaeur, Mel. Larimore, Taylor. LeBoeuf, Michael. The Bogleheads' Guide to Investing. Second Edition.

Mr. Money Mustache. The Shockingly Simple Math Behind Early Retirement. Mr. Money Mustache. 2012. https://www.mrmoneymustache.com/2012/01/13/the-shockingly-simple-math-behind-early-retirement/

NAPFA. "Americans Need To Understand What Financial Planning Is And How It Can Help: NAPFA introduces new infographic on the important role of financial planning." NAPFA. 2012. https://legacy.napfa.org/UserFiles/File/ImportanceofFinancialPlanningRelease100312.pdf

New Jersey Council For Economic Education. "Developing Economic and Financial Skills in New Jersey Students." New Jersey Council For

Economic Education. 2013. http://newjersey.councilforeconed.org/wp-content/uploads/sites/2/2013/11/NJCEE-Overview-2013.pdf

Pritchard, Justin. Are Credit Unions a Safe Place for Your Money? The Balance. 2019 https://www.thebalance.com/are-credit-unions-safe-315403

Ramsey, Dave. Housing Trends. Dave Ramsey. 2019. https://www.daveramsey.com/blog/housing-trends

Ramsey, Dave. Return on Investment; the 12% Reality. Dave Ramsey. 2020. https://www.daveramsey.com/blog/the-12-reality

Robbins, Tony. Money Master The Game. Simon&Schuster Paperback. 2016.

Royal, James. 10 Best Retirement Plans in 2020. Bankrate. 2020. https://www.bankrate.com/retirement/best-retirement-plans/

Stanley, J Thomas. Stop Acting Rich. Thomas J. Stanley. 2010. http://www.thomasjstanley.com/2010/06/stop-acting-rich-act-like-ken/

Endnotes

[i] NAPFA. "Americans Need To Understand What Financial Planning Is And How It Can Help: NAPFA introduces new infographic on the important role of financial planning." NAPFA. 2012.
https://legacy.napfa.org/UserFiles/File/ImportanceofFinancialPlanningRelease100312.pdf

[ii] New Jersey Council For Economic Education. "Developing Economic and Financial Skills in New Jersey Students." New Jersey Council For Economic Education. 2013.
http://newjersey.councilforeconed.org/wp-content/uploads/sites/2/2013/11/NJCEE-Overview-2013.pdf

[iii] Johnson, Angela. "76% of Americans are living paycheck-to-paycheck." CNN. 2013.
http://money.cnn.com/2013/06/24/pf/emergency-savings/index.html

[iv] Ramsey, Dave. Housing Trends. Dave Ramsey. 2019. https://www.daveramsey.com/blog/housing-trends

[v] Robbins, Tony. Money Master The Game. Simon&Schuster Paperback. 2016. Pg.93.

[vi] Kobliener, Beth. Get a Financial Life. Simon & Schuster. 2009. Pg.22.

[vii] Stanley, J Thomas. Stop Acting Rich. Thomas J. Stanley. 2010. http://www.thomasjstanley.com/2010/06/stop-acting-rich-act-like-ken/

[viii] Danko, D William. Stanley, J Thomas. The Millionaire Next Door. Taylor Trade Publishing. 2010. Pg. 3-4.

[ix] Danko, D William. Stanley, J Thomas. The Millionaire Next Door. Taylor Trade Publishing. 2010. Pg. 10-11.

[x] Danko, D William. Stanley, J Thomas. The Millionaire Next Door. Taylor Trade Publishing. 2010. Pg. 13.

[xi] Kobliener, Beth. Get a Financial Life. Simon & Schuster. 2009. Pg.33.

[xii] Kobliener, Beth. Get a Financial Life. Simon & Schuster. 2009. Pg.40.

[xiii] Kobliener, Beth. Get a Financial Life. Simon & Schuster. 2009. Pg.54.

[xiv] Pritchard, Justin. Are Credit Unions a Safe Place for Your Money? The Balance. 2019 https://www.thebalance.com/are-credit-unions-safe-315403

[xv] Pritchard, Justin. Are Credit Unions a Safe Place for Your Money? The Balance. 2019 https://www.thebalance.com/are-credit-unions-safe-315403

[xvi] Kobliener, Beth. Get a Financial Life. Simon & Schuster. 2009. Pg.87.

xvii Kobliener, Beth. Get a Financial Life. Simon & Schuster. 2009. Pg. 96-97.

xviii Mr. Money Mustache. The Shockingly Simple Math Behind Early Retirement. Mr. Money Mustache. 2012. https://www.mrmoneymustache.com/2012/01/13/the-shockingly-simple-math-behind-early-retirement/

xix Mr. Money Mustache. The Shockingly Simple Math Behind Early Retirement. Mr. Money Mustache. 2012. https://www.mrmoneymustache.com/2012/01/13/the-shockingly-simple-math-behind-early-retirement/

xx Lindaeur, Mel. Larimore, Taylor. LeBoeuf, Michael. The Bogleheads' Guide to Investing. Second Edition.

xxi Ramsey, Dave. Return on Investment; the 12% Reality. Dave Ramsey. 2020. https://www.daveramsey.com/blog/the-12-reality

xxii Hamm, Trent. Compound Interest Versus Inflation: The Battle For Your Money. The Simple Dollar. 2019. https://www.thesimpledollar.com/investing/blog/compound-interest-versus-inflation-the-battle-for-your-money/

xxiii Investopedia. Portfolio. Investopedia. 2020. https://www.investopedia.com/terms/p/portfolio.asp

xxiv Investopedia. Diversification. Investopedia. 2020.

https://www.investopedia.com/terms/d/diversificat
ion.asp

[xxv] Lindaeur, Mel. Larimore, Taylor. LeBoeuf,
Michael. The Bogleheads' Guide to Investing.
Second Edition.

[xxvi] Investopedia. The Basics of Bonds.
Investopedia. 2020.
https://www.investopedia.com/financial-
edge/0312/the-basics-of-bonds.aspx

[xxvii] Bernstein, William J. If You Can. William J
Bernstein. 2014.

[xxviii] Robbins, Tony. Money Master The Game.
Simon&Schuster Paperback. 2016. Pg.95.

[xxix] Kobliener, Beth. Get a Financial Life. Simon
& Schuster. 2009. Pg.104.

[xxx] Kobliener, Beth. Get a Financial Life. Simon &
Schuster. 2009. Pg.110.

[xxxi] Investopedia. ETF. Investopedia. 2020.
https://www.investopedia.com/terms/e/etf.asp

[xxxii] Royal, James. 10 Best Retirement Plans in
2020. Bankrate. 2020.
https://www.bankrate.com/retirement/best-
retirement-plans/

[xxxiii] Royal, James. 10 Best Retirement Plans in
2020. Bankrate. 2020.
https://www.bankrate.com/retirement/best-
retirement-plans/

[xxxiv] Royal, James. 10 Best Retirement Plans in
2020. Bankrate. 2020.
https://www.bankrate.com/retirement/best-
retirement-plans/

[xxxiv] Royal, James. 10 Best Retirement Plans in 2020. Bankrate. 2020. https://www.bankrate.com/retirement/best-retirement-plans/